THE
SABBATH
SOUL

Mystical Reflections
on the
Transformative Power
of Holy Time

Selection, Translation and Commentary by

E I T A N F I S H B A N E , Ph D

For People of All Faiths, All Backgrounds

JEWISH LIGHTS Publishing

Woodstock, Vermont

The Sabbath Soul:
Mystical Reflections on the Transformative Power of Holy Time

2012 Quality Paperback Edition, First Printing
© 2012 by Eitan Fishbane

Illustration on p. iv (JTSL MS 8269 [*Seder Tikkunei Shabbat*], fol. 35r) courtesy of The Library of The Jewish Theological Seminary.

Library of Congress Cataloging-in-Publication Data
Fishbane, Eitan P., 1975–
The Sabbath soul : mystical reflections on the transformative power of holy time / selection, translation, and commentary by Eitan Fishbane. — 2011 quality paperback ed.
p. cm.
Includes bibliographical references.
ISBN 978-1-58023-459-7 (quality pbk.)
1. Sabbath. 2. Time—Religious aspects—Judaism. 3. Rest—Religious aspects—Judaism. 4. Cabala. 5. Hasidism. 6. Spiritual life—Judaism. I. Title.
BM685.F528 2011
296.4′1—dc23

2011022641

10 9 8 7 6 5 4 3 2 1

Manufactured in the United States of America

Cover and Interior Design: Heather Pelham
Cover Art: "Beautiful Sunset on the Beach" © Shutterstock.com/FXQuadro

For People of All Faiths, All Backgrounds
Published by Jewish Lights Publishing
A Division of LongHill Partners, Inc.
Sunset Farm Offices, Route 4, P.O. Box 237
Woodstock, VT 05091
Tel: (802) 457-4000   Fax: (802) 457-4004
www.jewishlights.com

For my parents,
Mona Fishbane and Michael Fishbane

My lifelong teachers—
The home and the love that you gave us
showed me the beauty of Shabbat

ושותה כדי רביעית ויתן לכל המסובים ׃ זקודס
סיבלע על סתי ככרות יאמר ב״כ למבלע על
רפתא בכתוב לעיל בליל סבת ׃

(ויאכל וישתה בשמחה ובטוב לב)

ולאחר גמור הסעודה ילמד תורה ויזמר זמירות ל
לכבוד תפארת ועטרת ישראל ׃

זמירות ליום השבת

ברוך אדני יום יום ׃ יעמס לנו
ישע ופדיום ׃ ובשמו נגיל
כל היום ׃ ובישועתו נרים ראש עליון
כי הוא מעוז לדל ומחסה לאביון
שבטי יה לישרֵ׃ עדות ׃ בצרתם לו

Contents

Introduction   1

A Prayer for Joy *(LIKUTEI TEFILOT)*   11

Candle Lighting
(SEFER SEFAT 'EMET)   15

Longing for Closeness *(LIKUTEI TEFILOT)*   25

Spiritual Preparation
(PRI TZADDIK)   27

Freedom and Fear Transformed *(LIKUTEI TEFILOT)*   45

Wearing White on Shabbat
(PRI TZADDIK)   49

The Pleasure of Shabbat *(LIKUTEI TEFILOT)*   57

A Path through the Sea
(DEGEL MAḤANEH 'EFRAYIM)   59

The Desire for Money *(LIKUTEI TEFILOT)*   67

Soul of the World
(SEFER ME'OR 'EINAYIM)   69

Cleansing the Soul throughWashing
and Immersion *(LIKUTEI TEFILOT)*   85

CONTENTS

Kiddush
(*LIKUTEI HALAKHOT*)   89

An Intention for Eating on the Sabbath (*LIKUTEI TEFILOT*)   101

Eating and Contemplation
(*LIKUTEI HALAKHOT*)   105

Transforming Our Speech (*LIKUTEI TEFILOT*)   113

Ḥallah as a Symbol of Spiritual Wholeness
(*LIKUTEI HALAKHOT*)   115

Reading the Torah Portion as a
Spiritual Practice (*LIKUTEI TEFILOT*)   131

Refraining from Labor
(*LIKUTEI HALAKHOT*)   133

As Though All My Work Is Done (*LIKUTEI TEFILOT*)   145

Awareness of God
(*SEFER SEFAT 'EMET*)   147

Song and Peace (*LIKUTEI TEFILOT*)   157

Uniting the Physical and the Spiritual
(*SEFER SEFAT 'EMET*)   159

The Power of Melody (*LIKUTEI TEFILOT*)   169

Concluding Meditations   173
Acknowledgments   181
Notes   183
Suggestions for Further Reading   187

Introduction

We live in a world dominated by speed and distraction, with demands for our attention at every turn. We are conditioned to approach time as a reality to be managed for optimal productivity; so often we rush about our weeks with the frenzy of accomplishing and earning, worshipping the idols of egotism, pride, and greed. We are so consumed by that hunger for acquisition and expedition that we frequently forget the restorative blessing of stillness, our desperate need for rest. I speak not only of a rest from physical and emotional exhaustion—a rest that aims to recharge us for greater productivity and speed—but also of a rest that brings us back to the center of existence, a calm that allows us to reconnect with the divine breath at the soul of All. It is a spirit that we feel when we are in tune with the rhythms of our own breath. It is the Sabbath, the seventh day.

On the day of rest we are liberated from our enslavement to multitasking, from all of the electronic communication that pervades the six days of work. Unplugged from the world of commerce and the forms of connection that keep us at a remove from the living voice of the other, we are released into a zone of quiet and reflection—a time in which the calm of solitude can find perfect balance with the community and relationship of Sabbath life.

That is the true mystery of the Sabbath—the sublime secret that so many religious people already know intimately. But you need not be an adherent of a religious community to be moved by this message. Indeed,

1

I very much hope that you may also be reading this book as a spiritual seeker who simply struggles with the tensions posed by our all too work-driven world. I invite you in, hoping that the insights and messages of this volume may suggest a new way to understand your own spiritual practice. You may already share the view that our need for Sabbath rest is not a valorization of laziness and sloth (far from it!), but an awareness of the life-giving power of Shabbat. The seventh day is not for the sake of more work in ordinary time; it is for the Sabbath that we work and produce all week long.

On Shabbat, the world around us becomes still—all the demands and the heaviness that we carry are released. They will return soon enough, but on Shabbat we are able to step back, to look at our lives from a protected distance, from the warm interior of sacred time. It is the twilight glimmer of the sun in descent—the otherworldly texture of a time that is neither day nor night. The ancient Rabbis called this moment *"bein ha-shemashot"*—literally, "between the suns"—an instant that stands both within the arc of earthly time and decidedly beyond it. Masters of legal precision, these Sages sought to achieve unequivocal clarity as to when the sixth day (Friday) ends and the Sabbath begins. Beyond a carefully defined limit, the candles may no longer be lit, the food may no longer be cooked, words no longer written. But they were also well aware of that in-between time that we sense in our passage from the ordinary to the sacred, from *ḥol* to *kodesh*.

It is a time that whispers of mystery and redemption, a corridor within the hours that transports us to a new level of feeling and thought. All at once we are aware of the majesty that surrounds us like the cloth of a heavenly *tallit*; we are wrapped within a blanket of colors that reveals the entire spectrum in the blink of an eye. It is fullness and nothingness at one and the same moment; the world is created yet again, and all is at rest, in tranquility. It is the stillness of Jerusalem just before the siren sounds to announce the arrival of the Sabbath; when the heat of the day falls and the cool of evening approaches; when the cars are silent, and the walkers make their way in sublime quiet to their places of prayer. Meals are waiting to be shared in fellowship and love—until the door opens and it is all peace and joy, a Sabbath of peace.

The Sages of old spoke of Shabbat as a glimpse of the world to come—a gift to us human beings from the hidden treasure-house of God.[1] It is a time when we touch the realm of souls—that spiritual place both far beyond and deep within—when our lives are revealed as a pilgrimage, a quest for the heart of existence, the center and root in a sometimes rootless world.

On Friday night, as I place my open hands on my daughter's head, I am aware of the blessings given to me by my mother and my father each week of my childhood. I bless her and I can feel the unbounded energy of the countless generations that came before me—the organic bond of a people and an ancestry.

Shalom 'aleikhem, malakhei ha-shareit, malakhei 'elyon—Peace unto you, ministering angels of God, angels from above! You shining spirits from the divine world—dancing with the candle flames, present in the radiant faces of the children, washed and ready to receive the joy of Shabbat!

Ve-khulhon mit'atrin be-nishmatin ḥadetin—Then all Jews are crowned with new souls—*be-nehiru de-'anpin*—with faces shining with light from above.

This is how the *Zohar* describes the power of receiving Shabbat: we are, each and every one of us, infused with a new spiritual vitality, a new measure of soul. We are given the chance to be reborn each and every Friday eve—the universe opens to us with the gift of mystery and loving embrace, we are absorbed into the indescribable wonder of a world on fire with the love of God and the love of our fellow human beings.

On Shabbat we feel more alive than ever, more in tune with the immense beauties of ordinary living, with the glow born of true compassion and kindness, with the melody that sings at the heart of existence, that binds us to the great unbroken song of Being that has always been there—discovered again and again in each generation and in each new moment of genuine learning and hearing. With heart and soul opened to the One who breathes at the center of all life, we say the *Kiddush*—the blessing over the wine that seeks to gather all of our manifold blessings, scattered as they are in the dark terrain of our wanderings. And we gather them up into the *kos shel berakhah*, "the cup of blessing," the vessel that holds all of our hopes and yearnings for true renewal and transformation.

For as we recall the holiness that God emanated onto the seventh day—the sanctity of primordial Creation—we are also reminded of our own need to send the flow of blessing and holiness into this otherworldly day. So much depends upon us and our intention. All of those intentions, and all of those gathered dreams, fill the cup to overflowing—they are the moments of brokenness and pain that we bring from the week that has passed; they are the labors unfinished and the relationships unresolved. They are gathered into the cup of blessing, and they are lifted up in the moment of *Kiddush*—raised toward the redemption of the seventh day.

This is why the Friday night *Kiddush* speaks of two kinds of memory, two markers of who we are. These are *zeikher le-ma'aseh bereishit*—a remembrance of the act of Creation—and *zeikher le-yetzi'at Mitzrayim*—a remembrance of the exodus from Egypt. For on Shabbat we are aware of the mystery and wonder of Divinity that brings this world into being anew each and every day, the beauty that reminds us of the divine Source and our never-ending capacity for spiritual renewal and rebirth. And we are also always aware of how our experience of Shabbat is a *yetzi'at Mitzrayim*, an exodus from Egypt. For on Shabbat we are liberated from our enslavement to our physical selves—to our greed, our pride, our lust. On Shabbat we are reminded that deep down we are soul and spirit, the breath of divine speech, the song of divine yearning. And we must lift these two dimensions—renewal and freedom—to the gaze of a mind transformed, an awareness of the divine anchor that gives meaning and substance to our all too ephemeral time in this world.

Such is the way several hasidic masters read the words of Psalm 142:8: O God, please "liberate me from the imprisonment of my soul [*hotzi'ah mi-masger nafshi*]!" The Sefat 'Emet in particular (Rabbi Yehudah Leib Alter of Ger, d. 1904) understands this verse as a statement about the redemptive power of the Sabbath: the seventh day is a time of otherworldly freedom in which we are able to break free of the walls that constrain us during the six days of the week. In holy time we step outside of ourselves, beyond the *'anokhiyut*—the selfhood—of ordinary life, and we are able to experience the ultimate freedom of consciousness. This, the hasidic masters teach us, is the deeper meaning of Abraham's commanded journey in the book of Genesis: *Leikh leikha mei-'artzekha*, "Go forth from your land" (Genesis 12:1). What is this *'artzekha* of which the text speaks? In hasidic rhetoric, the *'artziyut*—literally, "the earthiness," or "the mundane"—is a term for the coarse physicality that keeps us from encountering the pure light of the sacred. And so, the journey of *leikh leikha mei-'artzekha* is a going forth from the limiting place of *'artziyut*—a liberation from the imprisoning forces of mundane concern and superficial obsession. Shabbat enables a new exodus for each and every one of us, stimulating our memory of the collective exodus from Egypt (*zeikher le-yetzi'at Mitzrayim*), and still making it present and personal. Go forth from the superficialities that enslave you, from the *'artziyut* that obstructs your ability to perceive the sacred all around. The soul's liberation coincides with the influx of the new Sabbath soul that descends from the upper realm on Friday eve. The soul of the workweek is transformed; the gates that imprison it are opened, and the restorative energy of the Sabbath soul is welcomed in.

Stepping out of our everyday physicality, we set out on a pilgrimage inspired by the journey of Abraham. The goal of this quest is "the land that God will show you [*ha-'aretz 'asher 'ar'eka*]" (Genesis 12:1)—in our adaptation, the holy Sabbath day, the redemption as it may be found and *seen* in this world. Entering into the sacred is a transformation of the terrain beneath our feet; we arrive in a new land of divine promise, a realm of time in which our sight has been elevated from the "eye of the body [*'ein ha-basar*]" to the "eye of the heart [*'ein ha-lev*]."[2] We now see with a spiritual sight, with a mode of perception lifted beyond the bounds of earthly experience, into the magical realm of an enlightened mind.

As we set out on our Sabbath walk to *shul* on Friday evening, let this be our *kavvanah*, our intention. With each step, wrapped within the wondrous shifting of day to night, the quiet of the week released into rest and holiness, we reenact the pilgrimage of Abraham our father— moving out of labor's thought with the conscious gesture of mindful walking, entering into the pathways of the eternal. The Sabbath walk is indeed our own pilgrimage to the center of Being, to the place where the rivers of divine light converge and emanate their vitality to all of existence. Such a physical journey is a highly spiritual practice: walking becomes an essential preparation for our approach to the divine presence, to stand before the Source of All with wonder, to open our mouths in prayer before the Life of the worlds.

❧

In an effort to explore the spiritual texture of the Sabbath, this book studies the writings of a range of mystical masters from the history of Hasidism—from the origins of the movement in late eighteenth-century Poland to the turn of the twentieth century. Heir to the legacy of medieval and early modern Kabbalah, Hasidism shifted the focus of reflection from the upper metaphysical realms of Divinity to the interiority of human spirituality and consciousness, to the psychological dimensions of piety. Instead of speculation directed toward the transcendent heavens above, the hasidic masters taught of a divine presence in this world, a theology centered in immanence and radical immediacy. God fills the earth as we know it, the earliest hasidic mystics emphasized— many explicitly asserting that God is nothing less than the oneness of all Being, that there is no real separation between Divinity and the rest of existence.

The texts have been arranged by theme, progressing for the most part in chronological order (exceptions to this rule include the pieces titled "Candle Lighting," "Spiritual Preparation," and "Wearing White on Shabbat"—drawn from the writings of two late nineteenth-century masters—an anomaly due to the fact that the content of these passages reflect ritual and contemplative points of entry into the Sabbath). This thematic progression seeks to evoke the movement of experience— advancing from candle lighting and the donning of white clothing to the Friday night *Kiddush* and the act of sacred eating. Such ritual-based themes are only part of the structure, however; I have also translated and interpreted sources that reflect a more amorphous spiritual transformation that takes place for the mystic on the seventh day—one in which the person undergoes a radical shift in awareness, a journey into the realm that is all soul.

I have selected each text from a wide landscape of Hebrew hasidic sources, offering both original translations and extended commentary. In addition, as part of an attempt to fashion a contemplative and devotional texture to the book, I have interlaced passages from the personal prayers of the Bratzlav (Breslov)* hasidic tradition (*Likutei Tefilot*—an anthology authored by Rabbi Natan of Nemirov, disciple of Rabbi Naḥman of Bratzlav)—selecting portions that express the spiritual dimensions of Shabbat in the language of devotional and individual yearning. These short prayers have been placed between each of the longer thematic selections, and with only one exception, I have translated them without any attendant commentary, in an effort to maintain their devotional character and to facilitate your contemplative experience of them. I encourage you to use these texts as centering moments of intention—integrations of the mystical ideas into the personal practice of your spiritual life.

The two earliest texts in this book (in terms of chronology) are drawn from the *Degel Maḥaneh 'Efrayim* (The Flag of the Camp of Ephraim) and the *Me'or 'Einayim* (The Light of the Eyes). The *Degel* is a classic of early Hasidism that reflects the teachings of Rabbi Moshe Ḥayyim 'Efrayim of Sudilkov (d. 1800), the grandson of Rabbi Yisra'el Ba'al Shem Tov, spiritual father of the hasidic movement in Eastern Europe. One of the masterworks composed in the golden era of first- and second-generation Hasidism, the *Degel Maḥaneh 'Efrayim* is a text that preserves

---

Publisher's note: Throughout this book the author uses the historical place-name and phonetic spelling *Bratzlav* for the name of the Ukrainian town where Rabbi Naḥman lived and taught between 1802 and 1810. However, the town's name is sometimes transliterated as Breslov, in accord with its Yiddish pronunciation. This spelling is used by the organization devoted to studying Rabbi Naḥman's legacy, the Breslov Research Institute, with which Jewish Lights has published several other books of Rabbi Naḥman's inspiring teachings.

core elements of the mystical teaching of the Ba'al Shem Tov (often shortened to Besht). *Sefer Me'or 'Einayim* derives from the same early period of hasidic creativity; it constitutes the teachings of Rabbi Menaḥem Naḥum of Chernobyl (d. 1797)—a disciple of the Ba'al Shem Tov—and also reflects the homiletic motifs of Hasidism's founding father. In the *Me'or 'Einayim* we encounter developed expansions on the Besht's central theme of radical divine immanence in the world; the heavenly derived Torah, the natural realm, and the human self are all understood to be inseparable parts of the ever-flowing divine life-force.

It was R. Moshe Ḥayyim of Sudilkov's nephew, however, who grew to even greater fame and influence. Rabbi Naḥman of Bratzlav, great-grandson to the illustrious ancestor of the hasidic movement, formulated a plethora of teachings pertaining to the mystical meaning of Shabbat. In the present book, we encounter these thoughts primarily through the transmission of Rabbi Natan of Nemirov, in his *Likutei Tefilot* (Collected Prayers) mentioned above as well as in his *Likutei Halakhot* (Collected Laws), a mystical commentary on Rabbi Yosef Karo's sixteenth-century classic of religious law, the *Shulḥan 'Arukh*. Both *Likutei Tefilot* and *Likutei Halakhot* reflect the disciple's attempt to adapt the teachings of the master in *Likutei Moharan* (Collected Teachings of Our Teacher, Rabbi Naḥman) to ritual halakhic and devotional contexts. Ever the faithful disciple, Rabbi Natan sought to fulfill his teacher's exhortation to make his teachings into prayers.[3] *Likutei Tefilot* attempts to do just that, taking different homilies from *Likutei Moharan* and transforming them into the spontaneous language of personal devotion and yearning. *Likutei Halakhot*, an eight-volume work, includes an extended unit given exclusively to the mystical meaning of the Sabbath; I have selected several rich passages from this rather vast corpus. As you will see upon studying them, these texts are among the most dense and symbolically laden passages that I have translated in this book. Rabbi Naḥman's teaching is notoriously difficult and run through with both kabbalistic symbolism and a complex thicket of associations. But the insights offered, which include spiritual intentions for the act of eating on Shabbat as well as the mystical depths of the *Kiddush* ritual, are among the most suggestive in the volume.

In preparing this work, I have sought to select from the writings of those hasidic masters who devoted the greatest attention to the subject of Sabbath holiness. For this reason, the texts collected here should not be construed to constitute a representative survey of hasidic literature more broadly; instead, it is a sampling of some of the greatest insights formulated by various hasidic mystics on the topic of Shabbat. Bearing this in mind, the texts move chronologically from early nineteenth-century Bratzlav to the late nineteenth-century masters of Lublin and Warsaw. Rabbi Tzadok ha-Kohen of Lublin (d. 1900) was one of the most prolific masters in the history of Hasidism, authoring a great range of works, including the seminal five-volume commentary on the Torah, *Pri Tzaddik* (Fruit of the Righteous One). A scholar of great learning both in the realms of classic talmudic study and in the mystical teachings of Kabbalah and Hasidism, Rabbi Tzadok was a master who evolved from the model of the *lamdan* (traditional, nonmystical scholar of rabbinic texts) to that of the charismatic mystic, while never abandoning the pervasive presence of his foundational Gemara learning.[4] *Pri Tzaddik* is particularly remarkable for our purposes, given that the first volume opens with more than one hundred pages devoted entirely to the subject of Sabbath holiness. The pieces that I have selected and translated from R. Tzadok's writings are but a small taste of the vast feast contained in this master's oeuvre, a sampling of the many insights offered in his treatise on *Kedushat ha-Shabbat* (Sabbath Holiness). These passages center on the process of spiritual preparation—the proper devotional attitude through which a person may become better able to receive the indwelling of divine holiness on the seventh day.

At the same time that R. Tzadok ha-Kohen was preaching and writing, another great hasidic master was also gathering a large following in a small town outside the Polish city of Warsaw. In Giora Kalwaria, known simply as "Ger" in Jewish sources, Rabbi Yehudah Leib Alter (d. 1904) served as a highly influential leader of hasidim, delivering the homilies each Shabbat that would eventually be published as *Sefer Sefat 'Emet* (The Language of Truth). It remains uncertain whether the text of the *Sefat 'Emet* was authored by the hand of the master himself or whether—like most works of hasidic homiletics—it was written down in Hebrew by faithful disciples after Shabbat, based on their memories of the original *derashah* as it was delivered in Yiddish. From remarks made on the title page of the *Sefat 'Emet*, it seems probable that the text was actually written by the rabbi's own hand, but we cannot say for sure. Either way, however, the *Sefat 'Emet* constitutes—along with the *Pri Tzaddik* of R. Tzadok ha-Kohen—one of the most remarkable pieces of hasidic literature from the later generations of the movement. Unlike the *Pri Tzaddik*, the *Sefat 'Emet* does not contain a treatise wholly devoted to the subject of the Sabbath, but it would not be an overstatement to claim that Shabbat is the motif and concern that runs through the entirety of all five volumes of the *Sefat 'Emet*, and the master returns time and again to this subject as the deep lesson of his broader spiritual teaching.[5] Often paired with his conception of the Sabbath, R. Yehudah Leib preached a bold theology of immanence—one in which Divinity is present in every element of Being as a contracted point of spiritual energy. He calls this the *nekudah temunah penimit*—the "inner hidden point," the spark of God that dwells in the deepest heart of each living being. And it is on Shabbat that we are able to access that inner point of Divinity, that portal to eternity and the mystery of all life.[6]

For the *Sefat 'Emet*, as for other hasidic mystics, the Sabbath is a time when we are able to break through to a new level of spiritual awareness and understanding; the path of religious cultivation is directed toward this goal. The spiritual life is an ongoing process of deep mindfulness, an opening up of consciousness to perceive the fundamental unity of all Being. Through Shabbat we may attain *behirut ha-da'at* (clarity of mind)— a state of awareness in which we are able to transcend our natural limitations, a level of thinking in which the organic oneness of all reality is manifest and the eternal presence of God is revealed.

It is my hope that this book will enrich your experience of the Sabbath—that the spiritual insights of the hasidic masters transmitted here will open new doors in your encounter with the day of rest. To paraphrase the *Zohar*, let us now enter into the mystery of the Sabbath, into the wonder and light of the seventh day!

A Prayer for Joy

May it be Your will—
our God and God of our ancestors—
that You might help me with Your great compassion,
and give me the merit to receive the holy Sabbath
with great joy and happiness,
delight, song, celebration, and gladness.

Guard and save me,
that no sadness or depression will befall my heart—
no sorrow and no lament,
no worry on the holy Sabbath day.

Let me only merit to rejoice
with all my strength on the holy Sabbath—
with all my heart, and all my soul and all my might—

With a joy that has no end and no limit,
as it is truly fitting to rejoice on the holy Sabbath—
on a day as holy and awesome as this,
when an immeasurable, great, and powerful joy
is awakened throughout all of the upper worlds
from the greatness of joy and delight
of the holy Sabbath below.

Rabbi Natan of Nemirov, *Likutei Tefilot* 2:13

Candle Lighting

1   **In the midrash it is taught.** *Bereishit Rabbah* 11:2.

2   **the inwardness is revealed.** The inner force is always present, pulsing at the center of Being. For the *Sefat 'Emet*, the *penimiyut* is the very presence of God—the life-breath of Divinity that dwells within. But during the six days of the week, we experience that life-force as through a veil of concealment, and only on Shabbat is it fully revealed to us.

3   **A man's wisdom lights up his face.** Ecclesiastes 8:1.

4   **This is the revelation of the extra soul.** Building upon earlier ideas, the medieval kabbalists articulated the notion that the Jew receives an "extra soul" on the Sabbath—a spiritual force that dwells within from Friday evening until *Havdalah* on Saturday night. Here the *Sefat 'Emet* attributes the glowing countenance of the Jew on Shabbat to the presence of that extra soul within. An influx of Divinity, the Sabbath soul is an entity of pure light descended from the celestial realm above.

5   **on the holy Shabbat.** The *penimiyut*—the divine force of inwardness—is not only found in the heart and soul of the person. It is also the life-force that dwells at the center of the world at large, at the core of Being itself. This is the primary way in which the *Sefat 'Emet* expresses the theology of radical immanence—a view that accords with the broader hasidic conception. God is not relegated to the transcendent heavens above; Divinity is to be found in the world below, in the realm of earthly and ordinary things. But just as the presence of God in the person is often concealed during the six days of the week, so too is that divine light revealed in the world on the holy Sabbath. God's presence is a force of light, and the sacred time of Shabbat opens our spiritual perception so that we may see that which is otherwise hidden from us.

6   **And there was light.** Genesis 1:3.

Sefer Sefat 'Emet

Rabbi Yehudah Leib Alter of Ger
Parashat Bereishit, teachings delivered in 1888

In the midrash it is taught[1]
that the light of a person's face during ḥol [the weekdays]
is different from the light of his face on Shabbat.
This means that on Shabbat the inwardness [penimiyut] is revealed,[2]
as it is written:
"A man's wisdom lights up his face."[3]

This is the revelation of the extra soul.[4]
And so too at large in the world,
the inwardness is revealed on the holy Shabbat.[5]
As it is written:
"And there was light [va-yehi or]."[6]

(continued on page 17)

7 **in the world to come.** This is an allusion to a highly influential passage in the Babylonian Talmud, Ḥagigah 12b, wherein the Rabbis assert that God first created a light so powerful and majestic that one could see through it from one end of the world to the other. But God became concerned that this pure light would be abused by the wicked, and so God hid that light away for the righteous in the time to come. And where did God hide that light? In the Torah, to be discovered anew in each generation by those who study the Torah with pure hearts.

8 **a portion of that light.** In this statement, the *Sefat 'Emet* has transformed the talmudic idea into the seed for an immanentist theology. The first light of Creation—the "*va-yehi or*"—was cloaked within the world at the dawn of time, and it remains there as the radiance of divine presence, waiting to be discovered by the spiritual seeker. Shabbat is that time of pure discovery, the moment when the veils of darkness recede and the light of Divinity emerges to full glow. The light *is* the divine presence; "all the work of Creation holds a portion of that light"—God is present in all the details of Creation.

9 **the *'aspeklaria* that does shine.** Here the Sefat 'Emet is alluding to the kabbalistic resonance of these phrases. Already in rabbinic literature a distinction is made between those prophets who see God through the *'aspeklaria she-'einah me'irah* (a darkened or cloudy lens) and the prophet Moshe, who alone saw God through the *'aspeklaria ha-me'irah* (the clear lens, the shining lens). In medieval kabbalistic symbolism, the *'aspeklaria she-'einah me'irah* refers to *Shekhinah*, the tenth *sefirah*, the feminine dimension of Divinity, and the *'aspeklaria ha-me'irah* refers to *Tif'eret*, the masculine dimension of Divinity.[1]

And our Sages of blessed memory taught that God hid that light
for the righteous in the world to come.[7]
The utterance "Let there be light"
is to be found in every detail of Creation—
for all the work of Creation holds a portion of that light.[8]

It has just been hidden,
and on Shabbat light is revealed from that concealed source.
During the six days of the week
that light exists in the sense of
the 'aspeklaria that does not shine [a darkened lens],
and on Shabbat it is like the 'aspeklaria that does shine [a clear lens].[9]

(continued on page 19)

10 **the Shabbat candles.** The candles shine with an otherworldly glow—a reminder of the radiant Presence that has begun to envelop us, transforming our ordinary space into a small sanctuary, a place made ready for God's dwelling.

God is the pure light that pulses at the core of Creation, the force of all that is. We yearn for that radiance in every unaware moment of our daily lives, crying out from the narrowness of superficial obsession. Slowly finding our way to the bright gleam of Divinity, like the lover and beloved of the Song of Songs, we leap over mountains in quest of the Heart of all hearts.

Most of the week we dwell in darkness—hovering over the face of the deep, unconnected to our spiritual Source. In that time, the time of the ordinary, the light of the divine face remains hidden in the innermost chambers of ourselves—it is unrevealed, and so often inaccessible.

Such is the light that was hidden in the Torah at the dawn of time.

And thus the lighting of the Shabbat candles[10]
is a *mitzvah* that hints to the revelation
of the hidden light on the holy Shabbat.

(continued on page 21)

11   **Though I sit in darkness, *YHVH* is my light.** Micah 7:8.

12   **the world to come.** In this passage from the *Sefat 'Emet*, Shabbat is presented as that time when the primal light of Creation is once again revealed. For, according to ancient tradition, Shabbat is a semblance of the world to come (*me-'ein 'olam ha-ba'*) that can be accessed while one is still in this world (*'olam ha-zeh*). It is a time when the transcendent wonder of all things is disclosed to the human eye, a time when the timeless sparkles with the shimmer of heaven, a moment when a portal to the immortal divine mystery is opened wide to our limited and mortal vision.

     It is on Shabbat that the first light of Creation shines through to us; each week we return to Shabbat as a source of warmth and illumination. And this is the hasidic reading of the midrash: a person's face glows in a fundamentally different way on Shabbat; on that day the full brilliance of Divinity is made manifest, that which is inward becomes revealed, and we are restored to the peace of primordial perfection.

13   **God called the light day.** Genesis 1:5.

14   **as it is written in the midrash.** See *Midrash Tehilim* 90.

15   **like yesterday that has passed.** Psalm 90:4.

16   **all the days of the week.** Already in the midrash, the two thousand years before Creation, when the Torah was created, are characterized as two great cosmic days. In the kabbalistic system, these two "days" refer to the *sefirot Ḥokhmah* and *Binah*. These two upper *sefirot* bestow the primal energy of Torah on the six "days of the week"—the six *sefirot* between *Binah* and *Shekhinah* (*Ḥesed, Gevurah, Tif'eret, Netzaḥ, Hod, Yesod*). *Binah* and *Shekhinah* are both understood to represent Shabbat within the divine realm, and the six sefirotic days between them are like the six days of the week sandwiched between two Sabbaths—the Sabbath that precedes the new week, and the Sabbath that follows the workweek. The primordial Torah is contained within *Ḥokhmah* (for what is wisdom, both the ancient Rabbis and the medieval kabbalists ask, other than Torah?), and that force of Torah—that primal hidden light—is sent down into the lower *sefirot* to be revealed on Shabbat.

The children of Israel anticipate the disclosure of the hidden light
as they feel the darkness of this world—
as it is written:
"Though I sit in darkness, *YHVH* is my light."[11]
For on the holy Shabbat, God be He blessed
reveals to us a semblance of the light of the world to come.[12]
As it is written:
"God called the light Day ... "[13]

The essence of characterizing "Day" and "Light" as "good"
is the Torah—
as it is written in the midrash:[14]
the Torah preceded the Creation of the world by two thousand years
...
which is to say: two days of Creation.
"For in Your sight a thousand years are like yesterday that has
        passed."[15]

And on Shabbat there is a revelation
from those two "Days";
Shabbat bestows *Ḥokhmah* [Wisdom] and *Binah* [Understanding]
upon the children of Israel for all the days of the week.[16]

(*continued on page 23*)

17 **If you would but heed His Voice.** Psalm 95:7.

18 **the voice of Torah.** The *Sefat 'Emet* teaches that the primordial divine light is present in the whole of Creation; it is a glow that dwells hidden beneath the surface of reality, and it is the same light that was concealed in the Torah.

The letters of Torah form the structure of the natural world—all of Being is nothing but the great speech of God. And so Shabbat is the time when the hidden light of Torah is revealed, when the garments of concealment are lifted and we stand in the presence of Divinity.

This, the *Sefat 'Emet* says, is the significance of reading the Torah portion on Shabbat: the reading and hearing of the sacred words release divine light into our midst—the first glow of Creation is sent into our hearts and souls on that day that is *zeikher le-ma'aseh bereishit* (a remembrance of the work of Creation).

What is more, we are given a beautiful *kavvanah* (intention) for the lighting of the Shabbat candles (*hadlakat ha-neirot*) on Friday night. Though we may feel that we wander in darkness during the week, Shabbat comes to light up our homes and our inner lives. Such is the way that the *Sefat 'Emet* reads the words of the prophet (Micah 7:8): "Though I sit in darkness, *YHVH* is my light" (*ki 'eisheiv ba-ḥoshekh YHVH 'or li*). During the week of ordinary time, we struggle to make a living and to accomplish our seemingly endless tasks. Sometimes this world can be a place of pain and great suffering; sometimes we can become mired in narrow and superficial thoughts. But Shabbat has been given to us as a precious gift of restoration and healing. As sunset arrives on Friday evening, as we breathe deeply and ignite the sacred flames of the Shabbat candles, the light of the world to come shines bright, and the radiance of the divine face eclipses all of our weekly worries. In this moment we are made whole again, and we are reminded of all that is good and sublime in this world.

For this reason there is a reading of the Torah on Shabbat,
as the light of Torah is revealed in that moment.
And thus did our Sages interpret the verse:
"If you would but heed His Voice this day"[17]
as referring to the holy Shabbat
through which [the Jews] can hear the voice of Torah.[18]

Longing for Closeness

Master of the world, what can I say before You?
For I know just how far I am from this!

And as great a level as this holy commandment and quality is,
such is the force of my distance from it—
and especially from the quality of joy on the holy Sabbath,
upon which nearly all depends,
and it is the essence of closeness to You.

Let me merit to draw the joy of Shabbat
onto the six days of the week,
until I am able to be joyous constantly,
with a true joy, even during the week!

Likutei Tefilot 2:13

Spiritual Preparation

1 **the days of creation.** We are ever in search for a glimmer of holiness in our lives—some redemption from the ceaseless flow of mundane time, of mundane things. We journey about in the desert of lost ways, in the clamored marketplace of acquiring and surviving, seeking and yearning to find our way back to the sanctuary of stillness, to the place of perfect beginnings, to the splendor of the divine face. Crossing that mysterious bridge from the wild shout of workday pressures to an otherworldly quiet, we return, we are restored.

Kedoshim tiheyu ki kadosh 'ani YHVH 'Eloheikhem, "You shall be holy, for I, *YHVH* your God, am holy" (Leviticus 19:2).

We breathe in, we breathe out—it is Shabbat. We are one with our breath. The sacred spirit of God—the *ruah* of all that is and will ever be—this fills our body and fills our soul. It is a stream of life that makes our days new, a *ruah kadosh* that sustains us and brings us back to our center, week in and week out.

2 **And he sanctified it.** Genesis 2:3.

3 **sanctified it Himself.** Rabbi Tzadok ha-Kohen teaches that this holiness—this center of our spiritual existence—depends upon both God and ourselves. In creating the world in six days and in resting on the seventh, God infused Shabbat with a cosmic force of holiness—a mysterious energy that lies present beneath the surface of things, that fills the air with divine love. That presence of God dwells in Shabbat for all time. Shabbat is not just a day as we know days in this world; it is an eternal vessel for the gift of divine influx and wonder, it is the very heart of the created world; indeed, it is the heart and soul of all reality. And so, before all else, it is God who bestows holiness onto the seventh day—it is both a remembrance of the work of Creation (*zeikher le-ma'aseh bereishit*) and the embodiment of an ongoing, unceasing process of making and renewing, the flow of divine life-force into the world all around and within us.

Pri Tzaddik

Rabbi Tzadok ha-Kohen of Lublin
1:7–8, 1:13

The holiness of Shabbat
was fixed and established by God, may He be blessed,
in that He sanctified it during the days of creation....[1]
For in the days of Creation it was said:
"And He sanctified it [va-yekadesh 'oto]"[2]
God, may He be blessed, sanctified it [the Shabbat] Himself.[3]

(continued on page 31)

4   **and to sanctify it.** Exodus 20:8.

5   **at the moment of its entrance.** God sends this holiness into Shabbat, and this powerful energy dwells deep within the shelter of the day. It endures there as an eternal presence. But it is not God alone who bestows holiness on this transcendent moment in time. The sanctity of the Sabbath also depends upon the actions of those who observe it.

6   **arousal from below.** What is that holiness that we encounter amid the ebb and flow of time? Why are we so drawn to it, and how does it change us?

Scholars of religion have long been fascinated with the idea of holiness. As a concept it has been understood to mark the foundations of the spiritual quest, of the perennial human discovery of the Divine, and the attempt to orient the patterns of daily life around that discovery. The presence of God erupts into human consciousness like a bolt of lightning that is here and then gone—our minds are opened in a moment to the infinite expanse of wonder and uncharted terrain. First we stand in darkness, asleep to the mysteries of the soul and the heart, and then an instant of light opens the way before us, shows us the road that will take us home again.

Home.

The moment of holiness is the opening of a portal where none appeared before; we can feel the closeness of God like the warmth of ocean air, like the mist of a woodland waterfall. It is the sublime realization that all cycles return to a center of existence, that we encounter the great mystery of life with palms opened to heaven. Suddenly we are there—present with our whole self, awake in a way that we have never been before.

7   **have consecrated you.** Exodus 31:13.

And nevertheless, when the Torah was given,
Israel was commanded to remember the Shabbat day
and to sanctify it [*zakhor et yom ha-Shabbat le-kaddsho*].[4]
For they must sanctify the Shabbat immediately
at the moment of its entrance.[5]

And this is the case
even though the essence of Shabbat's holiness
derives from God, independent of
any human action and arousal from below.[6]
And thus it is said about her [the Shabbat]
in *Parashat Ki Tisa*:
"You must keep My Sabbaths [*'et Shabbtotai tishmoru*],
for this is a sign between Me and you throughout the ages,
that you may know that I *YHVH*
have consecrated you [*ki 'ani YHVH mekaddishkhem*]."[7]
For God, may He be blessed,
also sanctifies Israel
by way of the sacred Shabbat that He has given to them.

(*continued on page 33*)

8   **not that they sanctify it.** Not only do Jews experience holiness on the Sabbath, but they also *become* holy through the Sabbath. Shabbat is the means by which God sends that heavenly gift called *kedushah* (holiness) into the vessel of the person in this world. We must approach the Sabbath with a posture of open reception, with an attitude of making ourselves ready to be transformed by the supernatural power of the day. For although we do act upon the day by engaging in a bestowal of sanctity (through the *Kiddush*), we are also receivers of a divine gift from above, open vessels into which the divine energies are poured, *keilim* (vessels) prepared to be elevated through the force of *kedushah*.

9   **a goodly gift.** Babylonian Talmud, *Shabbat* 10b.

10   **this is not the case.** Here there is an overt recognition of the fact that people are not all the same. We each have different talents and abilities, and just as we would acknowledge that a musical virtuoso possesses a heightened ability to hear and channel music, so too we may acknowledge that spiritual receptivity and perception vary from person to person. The individual who devotes him or herself to the refinement of the spiritual life, to the cultivation of an awareness attuned to Divinity, is able to sense the vibrations of holiness in a more magnified way than the individual unpracticed in these devotional arts.

11   **a person's worship.** Though we should note the double meaning of the word *'avodah* here—a term that can also carry the valence of "work."

And through their observance of Shabbat,
they too become sanctified—
through the sanctity of Shabbat.
It follows from this
that the Shabbat sanctifies *them* [the Jewish people],
and not that they sanctify it![8]

For this reason,
the Shabbat was called "a goodly gift,"[9]
for it is a gift that is bestowed
without any effort on the part of the person.
And so indicates the aforementioned verse:
"that I *YHVH* have consecrated you."
For from this we may discern that the sanctity of Shabbat
and its consequent bestowal of sanctity on the person
derives from God alone, may He be blessed,
without any arousal from below.

Nevertheless, this does not contradict the commandment
to sanctify the Shabbat that is incumbent upon *the person*.

And if it was due only to the sanctity that derives from God,
then all of Israel would be equal in their sensation of the holiness of
    Shabbat—
the ordinary person to the same extent as the priest.
And we have already mentioned in an earlier section
that this is not the case.[10]

Instead, the sensation of holiness is dependent
upon the manner of a person's worship ['*avodah*][11]
during the ordinary days of the week [*yemei ha-ḥol*]....

(continued on page 35)

33

12 **on that day.** According to R. Tzadok, there are different kinds of sensation and feeling that take place on the Sabbath, and the pleasure that we feel from resting, eating, and the like is not to be equated with a sensation of holiness. Holiness, the rabbi insists, is not just about feeling good, experiencing joy. It is not a purely physical experience, as is the pleasure we derive from the external enjoyments of Shabbat. It is interesting to note that R. Tzadok does speak about holiness in terms of "sensation" (*hargashah*)—a word generally associated with bodily feeling and experience. When we cultivate a prepared self during the week, we are then able to open the channels of spiritual sensation on the Sabbath; preparing to become a vessel for the divine indwelling enables us to "feel" the energies of Shabbat in a heightened and *meta*-physical way, a mode in which the spiritual dimensions beyond physical pleasure are received and integrated.

13 **a vessel ready to receive.** It is not just observance on the seventh day that is essential. It is the ongoing process of spiritual preparation that takes place during the ordinary time of the workweek. *Melakhah*, labor itself, must be approached with a mindful intention; all week long we work to prepare ourselves to become vessels of the sacred on the Sabbath. The time of work and the time of rest are bound together—they are interdependent, an organic unity. For only through *hakhanah*, through preparation, are we truly able to receive the influx of divine holiness on the seventh day. Then the person becomes a *mishkan*, a sanctuary for the presence of God; all week long we work to build the structure of that sanctuary, to craft the space in ourselves that is ready to absorb that transcendent light from above, that pure breath of Divinity that dwells at the center of Being.

What does it mean to view the workweek as preparation for holiness? How are we to take such lofty matters into the rush and frenzy of ordinary time?

The masses of people do not taste the holiness [of Shabbat] in their
    hearts;
they only sense their pleasure in resting from work [melakhah],
in eating and drinking—
despite the fact that this too is a commandment,
and they have fulfilled the injunction
to enjoy the pleasure of Shabbat [ve-kiyemu 'oneg Shabbat].

Nevertheless, this pleasure is unrelated to the sanctity of the day.
And with respect to what was said,
"that I YHVH have consecrated you"—
this refers to the sensation of the great ones of Israel
who sanctify and purify themselves, who desire the closeness of God,
who feel the holiness and the elevation of the worlds on that day.[12]

But even these great individuals are not equal amongst themselves,
and each one senses the sacred according to his level and his grasp,
each according to his preparation during the days of the week—
preparing for his approach to the sacred....
For even though the day itself is sacred to our Master,
nevertheless a person only grasps its holiness
to the degree that he has become a vessel ready to receive....[13]

And so, despite the fact that the essence of the Shabbat's holiness
already exists in itself
[owing to the fact that God bestowed holiness
upon it in the act of Creation],
nevertheless the Shabbat also needs human beings
to sanctify it [gam hu tzarikh benei 'adam lekaddesho].

(continued on page 37)

14   **the height of its holiness.** The Friday evening liturgy speaks to us of the Sabbath as a sheltering presence spread over us by the One who fills all things: *ha-pores sukkat shalom*, "the One who spreads a shelter of peace." That shelter, that peace, is the tapestry woven of our weekday deeds; our actions and intentions in ordinary time flow into our experience of the Sabbath.

The compassion that we give to our fellow human beings in pain, the justice and decency with which we conduct our business affairs, the ways we approach even the smallest of routine behaviors through the lens of spiritual intention—these all contribute to the formation of a self ready to serve as a vessel for the divine presence. We must not divorce our Sabbath lives from our workday lives. They are each essential parts of a whole self—a posture open to the eternal voice, alert to the resonance of an ancient music in our present.

15   **people grasp the rung of holiness through it.** This is a very striking and surprising statement: "All of the Shabbat's sanctity is that people grasp the rung of holiness through it." R. Tzadok here states in no uncertain terms that the ultimate purpose of the Sabbath is to effect a transformation in awareness within the Jew. The holiness of Shabbat is not a reality that has value in and of itself (in this formulation anyway); it rather serves a devotional end within the human experience. Opening the mind to the divine condition of holiness, allowing human consciousness to perceive that supernal force that is otherwise hidden from view—that is the instrumental purpose of Shabbat. The Sabbath was imbued with the properties of sanctity from time immemorial, but the entire aim of that infusion was and is its function in stimulating the elevation of spiritual consciousness and awareness for the Jew in the world.

This is to say,
according to the degree to which they are prepared
to receive its holiness
and to feel the holiness that flows
into the chambers of their hearts and their minds.
Through this the Shabbat day is sanctified,
in that it reaches the height of its holiness.[14]

But when a person is not ready to receive
[*ke-she-'ein 'adam mukhan lekabbel*],
he is like a person who does not exist.

For when individuals do not prepare themselves
for the receipt of holiness,
then the holiness is not revealed in the hearts of those persons,
and all of the Shabbat's sanctity
is that people grasp the rung of holiness through it
[*ve-khol kedushato hu she-yasigu benei 'adam bo madreigat ha-kedushah*].[15]

And thus,
according to the degree
to which a person prepares himself
to receive the holiness,
by this [measure] he sanctifies the Shabbat day.
This is the sanctification of the day—
what we say as blessing to God, may He be blessed—
that He sanctified us and sanctified the Shabbat.
This day is sanctified through the preparation
of ourselves to become holy.

16 **They blessed the manna ... as bread for two days.** *Midrash Bereishit Rabbah* 11:2. This is not a direct quote but appears to be based on formulations in *Midrash Bereishit Rabbah* 11:2; *Pirkei de-Rabbi Eliezer* 19; Rashi on Exodus 16:29; and, of course, the language of Exodus 16 itself.

Just as all of the work of Creation
needs repair [*tikun*] through human hands,
so too does the sanctity of the Shabbat day
need such a human *tikun*,
in that Shabbat is the completion of the days
of Creation and the rest that follows after the labor.

Even though its holiness is fixed and established
through the divine act of Creation,
it is still not in a state of complete revealed fixedness
in the heart of the person....

But after the effort of the days of the week
that follow in the service of God, be He blessed—
through the holiness of the preceding Shabbat,
and when the person merits to sanctify
the upcoming Shabbat
through remembrance and through his worship
during the ordinary days of the week—
then he merits the sanctity of Shabbat
in the revelation of his heart,
with a complete fixedness
that endures forever.

With respect to the blessing of Shabbat,
it is said:
"They blessed the manna
that fell on the sixth day [*ba-shishi*]
as bread for two days [*leḥem yomayim*],"[16]
and this blessing was on the sixth day.

(continued on page 41)

17   **any action whatsoever.** The mystics of old teach us that each of the seven days corresponds to a stage in the eternal flow and emanation of Divinity from the infinite depths to the life-force of our world. Each day in our time represents a progression within God's own self, a movement from the hidden to the revealed. The six days are inner divine forces that flow into the ocean of the seventh day; the Sabbath is the sparkling convergence of God's supernal life-force, the dimension that sends blessing and energy to our realm.

And so each moment of the week, here in the tumble and majesty of earth, speaks to us with the echo of transcendent mystery. If we can learn how to become attuned to its rhythms and melodies—if we can approach each ordinary moment as a possible opening into the sacred—then we take part in the building of the *mishkan*, the construction of the holy Tabernacle.

18   **blessing may come to dwell.** The spiritual force of divine blessing cannot descend into this world without a physical vessel to hold it. As the *Zohar* says in a famous passage (3:152a), just as angels cannot descend from heaven in their pure spiritual form, and souls cannot enter the world without a physical self to hold them, so too the spiritual essence of the Torah—originating in the divine realm, the *Zohar* teaches, from before the earth was created—required the outer garments of the text as we know it to hold that otherworldly spiritual core. So the same is said of the *berakhah* (blessing) that flows from Divinity into the mundane realm: the actions of human beings in cultivating preparation for the Sabbath fashion a vessel for the otherwise purely spiritual energies of divine blessing. Bodily existence is the structure that allows the divine spirit to manifest; it is always there, flowing with ceaseless energy, but it cannot be perceived unless there is a physical channel to hold it and bring it forth.

But the blessing does not reside in that day
because of itself [mi-tzad 'atzmo],
only because of what must take place in it
as preparation for the day of Shabbat
[hakhanah le-yom ha-Shabbat].

The blessing of Shabbat spreads forth,
is revealed and actualized through it.
Shabbat is called the source of blessings
[mekor ha-berakhot]
because every blessing in its essence
is devoid of any action whatsoever.[17]
And like the blessing of the manna on the sixth day,
when bread for two days fell,
the Israelites didn't take more from it to eat on the sixth day
than they took on every other day....

Rather it is that the descent and indwelling
of blessing is impossible in a place of emptiness
['iy 'efshar be-reikanaya],
and it requires an actual thing
and some action on the part of the person
upon which the blessing may come to dwell.[18]

For God, may He be blessed,
wants it all to be accomplished by the human being,
who is made according to the supernal model....

(continued on page 43)

19 **flows forth to them.** Thus there are two forces of energy in our worldly experience of time—that which flows from the Sabbath, and that which flows into the Sabbath. This is a lower reflection of the energies that flow from the *sefirah Binah* (the upper Sabbath within Divinity) and the energies that flow from the middle six *sefirot* (the six "days of the week") into *Shekhinah* (the lower Sabbath within Divinity). In answering the interpretive question—"Why does the Torah say both *va-yevarekh* [He blessed] and *va-yekadesh* [He sanctified]?"—R. Tzadok asserts that this doubling alludes to the twin dynamics of the Sabbath's relation to ordinary time. On the one hand, the Sabbath is shaped and impacted by the energies it receives from weekday time (the flow of *kedushah* energy), and on the other, the Sabbath sends forth energy—both to the week prior and to the week to come (the flow of *berakhah* energy).

And so, in the matter of the blessing
that is drawn from the source of blessings
of the seventh day,
it does not dwell and is not drawn
except by way of the action
performed during the six days of the week.

This is the distinction
between *kedushah* and *berakhah*—
kedushah/holiness is that which Shabbat receives
from the six days of the week,
and *berakhah*/blessing is that which Shabbat flows forth to them.[19]

Freedom and
Fear Transformed

Have compassion for me!
Help me merit to be joyous with a full heart
on the holy Sabbath—
that through this happiness I may pass from
slavery into freedom.

And through the joy and freedom of Shabbat,
let me expand and perfect my consciousness
with the greatest expansion and perfection,
all according to Your benevolent will.

And through this,
I pray that I might attain a state
of complete *yir'ah* [fear and awe]—
and that this *yir'ah* might dwell in my mind
without any foolishness whatsoever.

(continued on page 47)

1 **whom should I dread.** Psalm 27:1.

Only You will I fear—
my fear of You will be upon me
so that I do not sin.
And I will not fear anything else in the world—
the verse will be manifest in me, as it is written:
"God is my light and my redemption,
whom should I fear?
God is the stronghold of my life,
whom should I dread?"[1]

Likutei Tefilot 2:13

Wearing White
on Shabbat

1   **for each person.** If, during the week, clothing symbolizes our vanity and obsession with outward perception, the Sabbath has the power to transform our relationship to the garments we wear. For in the splendor of the seventh day, our clothes carry the potential to remind us of the holiness that we have entered. Each of us receives that sanctity in a different way—we are each unique vessels for the flow of divine blessing. What was just yesterday an anchor to the slavery of materialism has today become a marker of a new consciousness, a mind elevated to the wonder of Creation. On Shabbat, even the wearing of clothes can become a spiritual practice of great power: the very tangible act of wearing special garments holds the potential to open us to a new mindfulness. In the moment of wrapping ourselves in symbolic white, we are made aware of the shift in time that has taken place—the new spiritual dimension that has been drawn into this world. And white evokes the erasure of our ever-present materiality, the transcendence of our constant need to accumulate the things of this world. We enter into the fountain of spiritual cleansing—the Source that pulses beneath the Being of our universe, imbuing it with life from the infinite realm beyond.

Pri Tzaddik

Rabbi Tzadok ha-Kohen of Lublin
1:40–42

Ordinary clothes do not reflect the essence of a person,
for what special character do those clothes
have for a person if tomorrow someone else might wear them
and he might wear other clothes?

But Sabbath clothes—
which a person wears in honor of
the holiness of Shabbat in his midst—
surely they correspond uniquely to the person wearing them,
and according to the Sabbath holiness
that is fixed within him—
a sanctity that is surely also different for each person.[1]

Just as in the world to come
each person will have a world unto himself,
so too on Shabbat
a sanctity that resembles the world to come
is fixed in the hearts of the children of Israel—
each one unto himself,
each according to that which befits the root of his soul.

(continued on page 53)

2   **as is known.** On Shabbat we reach toward the radiance of that other world, to the time of redemption. Within the bounds of the seventh day we touch the boundless—the infinite light that nourishes and sustains the All of existence. And so the white garments that we wear on the Sabbath remind us that this here is the portal to heaven— planted in the world like the foundation of Jacob's ladder, reaching all the while to the heights above. The Sabbath is the channel by which we ascend to the *shemeimi* (the heavenly, the *shamayim*) while still grounded here on the earth (*ha-sulam mutzav 'artzah ve-ro'sho magi'a ha-shamaimah*). In the shelter of Shabbat, we are each of us likened to the high priest in the holy of holies—our white garments draw that energy inward and lift us higher. Perhaps it is a purity of spirit that is the Sabbath quest: our clothes resemble the white worn by the high priest in his moment of greatest purification; they resemble the ethereal garments of light worn by the souls who dwell in the realm above. When we shed the ordinary clothing of the workweek, we symbolically shed the encasement of our physicality, the skin of our materialism. The cleansing of our bodies—the washing through which we prepare to receive the Sabbath—is a marker for a spiritual cleansing and transformation that takes place in the twilight crossing of Friday eve. And the white clothes represent our acceptance of the new soul that has come to dwell upon us: in this moment we are filled with the spirit of divine beauty and love, reborn into the seventh day.

3   **will be your partner.** *Midrash Bereishit Rabbah*, 11:8.

And just as the holiness resembles the world to come,
so too the garments that a person wears in honor of that holiness
resemble the garments of the world to come.
For it is known that then too there are garments for the souls,
made out of Torah and *mitzvot*.

Because of this our Sages wrote that we should wear white clothes on
   Shabbat—
for these resemble the garments of the world to come
in which the righteous wear white.
The high priest on Yom Kippur,
which is the secret of the world to come
[*she-hu' sod 'olam ha-ba'*],
also wore white, as is known.[2]

On Shabbat, a person wears the garment of a groom [*levush ḥatanim*].
As our Sages already said:
"The Holy One, blessed be He, said to Shabbat,
'The Assembly of Israel will be your partner.'"[3]
She is the bride-queen and they are the groom who resembles a king—
all of Israel are the children of kings,
and they are called a "kingdom of priests"
by virtue of the fact that they are a holy nation
consecrated and wedded to the Sabbath—
she who is the dimension of royalty and queen.

(continued on page 55)

4   **the garments of priesthood.** Shabbat is characterized here and else-where as the bride dressed in her wedding finery, for the Sabbath itself is understood to embody the feminine presence of God—the *Shekhinah.* In this explanation, the wearing of white reflects the role of the Jew as lover of the Divine, spouse of the *Shekhinah.* To be dressed in white garments is to prepare to enter into the wedding canopy of love between person and God, the union of this world and the upper realm of Divinity. In the white clothes of marriage, we call out in love to the approaching bride of Shabbat: *Bo'i kalah, bo'i kalah—penei Shabbat nekabbelah!* "Come, O Bride! Let us receive the face of Shabbat!"

5   **the custom of Rabbi Yehudah bar Ila'i.** Babylonian Talmud, *Shabbat* 35b.

6   **an angel of the Lord of Hosts.** In this culminating moment of the text, R. Tzadok brings us back to a classic image from rabbinic litera-ture: the comparison of the Sabbath garments to the appearance of a heavenly angel. Though it is not stated directly in the passage from Tractate *Shabbat*, the implication is that Rabbi Yehudah bar Ila'i resembles an angel because of the special white garment that he wears entering into the Sabbath. It is a sacred garment that is worn immediately following the cleansing of the physical body ("he would wash his face, hands, and feet, and he would sit and wrap himself in fringed garments")—the person passes from the all too corporeal nature of the workweek into the angelic and wholly spiritual state of the Sabbath. At the threshold of Shabbat, we greet the supernal angels (*Shalom 'aleikhem malakhei 'elyon!*) and we are ourselves trans-formed into refractions of that angelic presence. Donning the pure garments of white, we are lifted beyond the boundaries of this world, into the ethereal light of the angels—standing in the restorative pres-ence of Divinity.[1]

The bride wears the adornments
through which she is recognized to be a bride,
and the groom wears the garments of a groom
through which he beautifies the image of a priest [*kohen*],
dressed in the garments of priesthood.[4]

For he is not called a priest
in his priestly function without them,
insofar as they are the garment for that holiness
that God be He blessed sent into the priests
in the context of their worship.

It is this same holiness
that all of Israel merit to taste on the Sabbath day,
for at that time they are like a groom—like a priest.

And Sabbath clothes are like the clothes of priesthood
[*bigdei Shabbat heim dugmat bigdei kehunah*].

Thus did our Sages say that this was the custom
of Rabbi Yehudah bar Ila'i:[5]
"Before the Sabbath they would bring him warm water
and he would wash his face, hands, and feet,
and he would sit and wrap himself in fringed garments,
resembling an angel of the Lord of Hosts."[6]

The Pleasure of Shabbat

Master of the world, full of compassion—
the One who is good
and brings goodness to all—
let me merit to truly taste
the pleasure of Shabbat.

Likutei Tefilot 2:13

A Path through the Sea

1   **on the first of the month it shall be opened.** Ezekiel 46:1.

2   **a path through mighty waters.** Isaiah 43:16. Even before we delve further into the way the master develops this analogy, we may marvel at the illuminating lens through which he has set out to clarify the distinction between holy time and ordinary time. The rebbe of Sudilkov has juxtaposed Ezekiel 46:1 and Isaiah 43:16 in a vision of Shabbat as a redemptive pathway amid a powerful and otherwise overwhelming ocean of experience. Our lives in ordinary time, within the struggles of the workweek, are likened to the turmoil of raging waters; it is the Sabbath that offers both a respite from that tumult and a way through—a crossing of the *mayim 'azim* (mighty waters) of *ḥol*. The tone of the phrase *ha-notein ba-yam derekh* (He who provides a road through the sea) also evokes an initial sense of disorientation, of feeling lost—the redemptive act of divine intervention is to provide a "road through," a finding of the way when the sea feels vast and unconquerable.

3   **blessed is God, and blessed is His name.** It is this world that feels like a disorienting sea, a place in which we find our way through the gift of a divine pathway. The experience of mundane life, the challenges of trying to live spiritually amid the distractions and desires of physicality—this we try to anchor to those all too ephemeral moments of connection to our divine Source, our center and compass in a frequently overwhelming wilderness. But the rabbi does not reject the physical at all. To the contrary, we must seek to find the presence of the Holy One in all the matters and affairs of our very bodily existence; the challenge is to discover spiritual meaning and divine depth even in the places where we thought none dwelled. Each and every moment must be transformed into a portal to the One "whose Glory is the fullness of the earth." Those moments lift the stream of ordinary consciousness to a higher plane of spiritual awareness and perception, and it is in those moments that we realize the pathway that has been carved for us from the raging seas of mundane life. The formation of this *derekh* (road) is a crossing through the ocean of undifferentiated mind, the sudden epiphany that God is the great All of Being, the fullness of existence and its interconnected web of life.

(continued on page 62)

Degel Mahaneh 'Efrayim

Rabbi Moshe Ḥayyim 'Efrayim of Sudilkov
Likutim, beginning with *"Koh 'amar"*

"Thus said *YHVH*:
'The gate to the inner courtyard
that faces east [*ha-poneh kadim*]
will be closed during the six days of the week,
but on the Sabbath day it shall be opened,
and on the first of the month it shall be opened.'"[1]

This may be interpreted along the lines of:
"He who provides a road through the sea
and a path through mighty waters
[*ha-notein ba-yam derekh, u-ve-mayim 'azim netivah*]."[2]
For this world,
in all of its matters and affairs,
resembles a sea.
And when a person finds, in all of his physical affairs,
the Holy One, blessed be He,
whose Glory is the fullness of the earth,
then he effects a unification, as it were—
blessed is God, and blessed is His name.[3]

(continued on page 63)

The expression "then he effects a unification, as it were" is an allusion to the older kabbalistic practice of stimulating positive effects within the divine self through sacred human actions (and unifications of the various *sefirot* that make up God's inner life). The usage here seems to have a different connotation, however—though the precise meaning of effecting a unification (*'oseh sham yiḥud*) is unclear in this context. It would appear to carry the implication of achieving a transformed state of spiritual awareness, a heightened consciousness of the pervasive nature of the divine presence in the earthly realm. In this text, as in several others that we study in this book, the Sabbath is framed as a time in which the human mind is able to reach a greater plane of mystical attunement—a domain of experience in which the traces of Divinity emerge from their concealment, rising to awareness as a form of spiritual revelation. The mode of being described here by the Sudilkover rebbe is one of disciplined mindfulness to the ways in which God fills each moment of our ordinary physical lives. It is just so hard to achieve real awareness of this Presence—and so the Sabbath comes to break open the shells of our perception, to part the tumultuous waters of mundane experience, to lead us into a reborn state of spiritual consciousness.

4   **the righteous ones will pass through it.** Psalm 118:20.

5   **You made them all with wisdom.** Psalm 104:24.

6   **He established the earth with wisdom.** Proverbs 3:19.

During the six days of *ḥol* it is difficult to reach this level,
except for men of God,
masters of knowledge [*da'at*] and the soul.
But on Shabbat it is easy for all people to reach that level,
and thus did God command us to eat and drink
and take pleasure on Shabbat—
for on Shabbat everything is unified [*nityaḥed ha-kol*],
and this is the inner gate [*sha'ar ha-penimit*]
that faces east [*ha-poneh kadim*],
which we may interpret in the sense of
"This is the gate to God—
the righteous ones will pass through it
[*zeh ha-sha'ar le-YHVH, tzaddikim yavo'u vo*]."⁴

That is to say:
We should bind together all the physical matters,
and gather them to their roots
through the inwardness that they have
within themselves [*mi-tzad penimit she-yeish bo*].

This is the meaning of
"You made them all with wisdom [*kulam be-ḥokhmah 'asita*]"⁵
and "He established the earth with wisdom [*be-ḥokhmah yasad 'aretz*]."⁶

(continued on page 65)

7 **His kingship rules over all.** Psalm 103:19.

8 **primarily directed to Wisdom.** Here the Sudilkover rebbe has offered a wonderful interpretive play in order to convey his powerful spiritual teaching. What does the phrase *ha-poneh kadim* ("that faces east") teach us about the practice of a spiritual life? Instead of understanding the verb *poneh* as referring to the geographical direction of the inner courtyard and gate of the future Temple (as is the literal meaning of the verse from Ezekiel), the *Degel Maḥaneh 'Efrayim* understands it as a reference to the spiritual gaze of the person. When you "face" the things and places of this world—when you turn your gaze to them—always remember to maintain awareness of their rootedness in the divine Source. The word *kadim* is transformed in this interpretation: in the original biblical verse, it means "east," but the word can also mean "primarily" or "first." And such is the way that the hasidic master chooses to read it in order to dramatize his homily. In all of your experiences and encounters in the world, you should seek to attune your mind to the deeper mystical wisdom of the reality you behold. Ordinary being and physical existence are filled with the hidden presence of God; we just need to cultivate a refined state of spiritual consciousness in order to perceive it.

The child is like the father,
for "His kingship rules over all [*malkhuto ba-kol mashalah*]."[7]
And this is the meaning of
"that faces east [*ha-poneh kadim*]"—
that is, all of the ways in which you turn [*kol pinot she-atah poneh*]
and direct yourself in the world
should be primarily directed to Wisdom [*kadim le-ḥokhmah*].[8]

The Desire for Money

Through the holiness of Shabbat
let us merit to break and nullify
the desire for money from our midst,
that we not have any appetite or desire
for money whatsoever.

Let us only desire and yearn
for the eternal goal, always:
to be adorned for the day that is entirely Shabbat
and rest for life everlasting.

Likutei Tefilot 1:49

Soul of the World

1   **first fruits of His harvest.** This formulation is based on the wording of Jeremiah 2:3. Early midrashic interpreters (most notably at the beginning of *Bereishit Rabbah*) offered several different creative readings of the first line of Genesis, each centering on a deconstruction of that first word in the Torah—*bereishit*. In reading *bereishit* as "for the sake of Israel," these midrashists understood the word *reishit* as a stand-in for *Yisrael*, building upon the language of Jeremiah mentioned above: "Israel was holy to *YHVH*, the first fruits of His harvest." Thus armed with another valence of this opening scriptural word, the ancient Rabbis were able to read the line *Bereishit bara' 'Elohim 'et ha-shamayim ve-'et ha-'aretz* as, "For the sake of Israel (*bishvil reishit*) did God create the heavens and the earth.

2   **for the root that is the Creator blessed be He.** The hasidic master here offers a further spiritual twist on the ancient midrashic exegesis. God created the heavens and the earth for the sake of Israel, *so that the people Israel would worship God with a great love and intensity*. At this point, R. Menaḥem Naḥum introduces the key mystical terms *devekut* (attachment) and *teshukah* (yearning), markers of a heightened state of devotion. In this framing, much like in Abraham Joshua Heschel's classic *God in Search of Man*,[1] the world was created as an expression of the divine desire to be loved. The Holy One yearns to be yearned for; the purpose of existence is for that very reality to express love and longing for its source.

    The ideal of devotion is here formulated as the height of spiritual love. Like the pietists of older times, our homilist speaks of a paradigmatic state of worship in which we give our hearts to divine service, in which the life of prayer, *mitzvot*, and contemplation are marked by the arousal of a powerful yearning from deep within—a cry for the divine beloved that echoes the overflowing love expressed in the Song of Songs. The challenge of our religious lives thus becomes the difficult process of purifying our hearts of anger and animosity, and releasing ourselves from the terrifying power of fear. Only then can we truly progress from *yir'ah* to *'ahavah*—from fear to love— a posture that is directed to God in many ways, most tangibly through

(continued on page 72)

Sefer Me'or 'Einayim

R. Menaḥem Naḥum of Chernobyl
Parashat Ki Tavo

It is known that the world was created for the sake of Israel,
as it is written (Genesis 1:1):
"In the beginning *'Elohim* created" [*bereishit bara' 'Elohim*].

For the sake of Israel, who are called
"the first fruits of His harvest" [*reishit tevu'ato*],[1]
for the whole intention of the Creator blessed be He
in the creation of the world was for the sake of Israel,
so that they would worship with a perfect devotion,
with attachment [*devekut*] and a great yearning
for the root that is the Creator blessed be He.[2]

(*continued on page 73*)

the manifold faces of human encounter and relationship that test and form us on a daily basis. As our character is gradually uplifted through genuine patience and compassion, we are readied for revelation and *devekut*. Only when the heart has been purified of our moral obstacles are we able to open ourselves, vulnerable and filled with *teshukah* [yearning], to the life-altering love of God.

3 **Israel nourish their Father in heaven.** As a direct source, this phrase does not seem to appear prior to the sixteenth century in the writing of R. Elazar Azikri [*Sefer Ḥareidim* 66] (and then in a more widespread fashion in hasidic literature), but it is clearly based on a related formulation in *Midrash Zuta Shir ha-Shirim* 1, in which the homilist states that when a person gives charity to the poor, he is also supporting and nourishing the Holy One blessed be He, a wonderful theological framing of the act of giving *tzedakah*.

4 **do not separate from Him, may He be blessed.** Like the theurgical drama of kabbalistic thought, the hasidic master here underscores the way in which the actions of human beings affect and impact God. Divinity is infused with delight and is nourished by the degree to which Jews draw closer in devotion. Here it is the act of coming closer, the commitment to a full and complete unity that nourishes the divine Self.

5 **to draw close to one another.** Is the distance between person and God an unbridgeable chasm? Can we, as limited and finite creatures, touch that which is infinite and immortal? The heart of the religious quest is our journey toward the mystery that lies just beyond the edges of the human mind. In the moment of devotion, in the expression of spiritual yearning, we seek to encounter a reality that is beyond ourselves, an essence that dwells in the depths. In the classical model of the transcendent God, the nature of Divinity lives beyond our reach— our bounded existence is incompatible with the exalted character of the celestial realm. This was the belief of the great Jewish philosophers of the Middle Ages, among them Rabbi Saadia Gaon and Rabbi Moses Maimonides. Because of our physical and finite natures, we cannot know and experience the supreme mystery of God's existence. But

(*continued on page 74*)

And through this they bring about delight and yearning
in the Creator blessed be He, as it were,
for the Creator receives great delight from
the actions and worship of the lower realm,
more than from the heavenly hosts,
as it is written:
"Israel nourish their Father in heaven"
[*yisrael mifarnesim le-'avihem she-ba-shamayim*].[3]
They infuse Him with delight, as it were [*kivyakhol*]—
they do this when they draw closer in complete truth
and do not separate from Him, may He be blessed.[4]

It just must be understood
how they can achieve attachment and knowledge—
for is not the Creator blessed be He without end and boundary
and the human being a bounded and finite creature?
How is it possible for two such opposites
to draw close to one another?[5]

(*continued on page 75*)

the mystics—starting with the kabbalists of medieval Europe and continuing through to hasidic masters like R. Menaḥem Naḥum of Chernobyl—asserted that we can, and indeed we must, reach toward the brilliant light of God's infinite being. The heart of the religious path, and indeed the deepest purpose of our lives, is to worship God with a soul aflame, to attach ourselves to the divine light in complete *devekut* and unity.

6 **must resemble both aspects.** Shabbat stands on the border of existence, between the physical and the spiritual, between earth and heaven. The finite nature of the human being precludes access to the infinite—they are opposites and incompatible. But out of a great love, and from a powerful yearning to be loved in return, God gave the Jewish people the Sabbath as a bridge between orders of reality. As we will see below, Shabbat is divine in origin, but brought into this world to be inhabited by mortal creatures. Because of this dual nature, the Sabbath functions as a vehicle for that ideal devotional attachment and unity of human and deity.

7 **As it says in the *Zohar*.** *Zohar* 2:88b.

8 **the life-force of this world.** The assertion that Shabbat is the name of God is particularly significant here, owing to the pervasive mystical claim that the divine name is part of the very being of the divine Self.[2] In kabbalistic theology, the intradivine realm of the *sefirot* was also represented according to the structure of the ineffable four-letter name of God: the letter *yod* correlates to the *sefirah Ḥokhmah*; *heh* corresponds to the *sefirah Binah*; *vav* to the middle six *sefirot*; and the last *heh* to *Shekhinah*. The name was understood to be an inscribed representation of the Being and emanation of God. To speak of the Tetragrammaton was to speak of the divine essence, and to attach oneself to the holy name was to bind oneself to the life of God. Thus, to say that "Shabbat is the name of the Holy One" is to assert that the Sabbath is a metaphysical, heavenly entity that is part and parcel of the divine Self. There is no fundamental separation between God and the Sabbath; to attach oneself in devotion to Shabbat is to become attached to the divine name—it is to be bound and united with the divine life-force as it manifests in this world.

For this reason did the Creator blessed be He give the Sabbath to
    Israel,
for the Sabbath is an intermediary between
Israel and their Father in heaven.
It unites and binds them to the Creator blessed be He
because it contains both parts,
and it therefore resembles both Israel and the Holy One.
For it is known that something that is located in between two
    opposites
must resemble both aspects [beḥinot].[6]

As it says in the Zohar,[7]
Shabbat is the name of the Holy One blessed be He
[Shabbat sheima' de-kudsha brikh hu']—
perfect and complete on all sides—
for Shabbat is the life-force of the upper world [ḥiyut 'olam ha-'elyon]
and the life-force of this world.[8]

(continued on page 77)

9   **the seventh day that exists in this world.** As we saw in the writings
of the *Sefat 'Emet* and the *Pri Tzaddik* (though we should recall that the
Me'or 'Einayim is much earlier chronologically), Shabbat is here understood to be the animating force within ordinary time; the Sabbath is
like the soul to the body of the six days of the week. This construction
of the seventh day as the cosmic life-force (*ḥiyut*) stems from the
notion that Shabbat itself is an extension of the very being of God.
There is an ontological reality to this window in the stream of time—
it is a spiritual substance that is emanated from the divine Self. As we
observed earlier, Shabbat in this world is a lower manifestation of a
reality that exists within Divinity: our experience of the Sabbath is
an indwelling of the divine *sefirot Binah* and *Shekhinah*. Shabbat as we
know it in our realm is nothing less than the presence of God.

It is for this reason that our attachment to the Sabbath holds the
power to bring us to an otherwise inaccessible encounter with the
heavenly realm. Shabbat is one of the most vibrant and immediate
ways in which we experience divine light and mystery on the earthly
plane. It is the infusion of a nourishing soul and spirit in the sometimes parched terrain of physical existence. In the mystical tradition,
the human soul is believed to originate in the divine domain. Indeed,
it is understood to be a spark of that primordial divine light, and
therefore of the same essence as Divinity itself. It is for this reason
that the soul is believed to be eternal and immortal: while the body is
finite and bounded, the soul descends from the Being of God. Thus,
the Sabbath and the soul are both portions of the divine life-force.
They are each extensions and emanations from the fountain of
supernal divine reality. Derived from the same eternal Source, they
are compatible with divine infinity in a way that physical and mortal
elements are not. The soul inhabits and animates the human body;
the Sabbath dwells within the shell of ordinary time and existence,
endowing it with vitality and sustenance. In binding our souls to the
Sabbath, we are able to reach toward the eternal divine light with
the force of *devekut*, to transcend our physical human limitations.

10   **Thus is it said.** Exodus 31:14.

It is the emanation of His glory, blessed be He,
which flows down and contracts itself into
the seventh day that exists in this world.[9]
The seventh day, which we call Shabbat,
is like a body and a garment
for the supernal Sabbath day,
which is the name of the Holy One.

The supernal Sabbath [*Shabbat 'ila'ah*]
is the soul of the entire world [*nishmat kol ha-'olam*] ...
For the supernal Sabbath contracts into [the seventh day below],
and it is the life-force of all the world.
Thus is it said:[10]
"He who profanes [the Sabbath] shall be put to death"
[*mehalilehah mot yumat*].

(continued on page 79)

11 **if someone slain is found.** Deuteronomy 21:1.

12 **the language of the taking of a soul.** Recalling this relic of biblical theology and punishment for the violation of the Sabbath, the Chernobyler rebbe correlates the word *meḥaleil/ḥilul* [profanation] to another use of this root in Deuteronomy 21—*ḥalal* as the dead or slain individual. Much like the interpretive wordplay that we will soon observe in the writings of Rabbi Natan of Nemirov (transmitting the teachings of Rabbi Naḥman of Bratzlav), in which the meaning of *ḥalal* as empty space is used to evoke the absence of divine presence that is caused by a profanation of the Sabbath [*ḥilul Shabbat*], this passage from *Me'or 'Einayim* evokes the image of absence and emptiness. The life-force of the Sabbath is said to withdraw in response to such *ḥilul Shabbat*—the animating soul of Divinity flees from the space of violation, and the physical shell that remains obtains the category of death and lifelessness. We are drained of spiritual nourishment and energy when our posture is robbed of an alignment with the sacred. Holiness is the fountain of renewal and animation: when we forsake the wonder of the divine Source, when we cease to discover the radiance and mystery that pulses at the core of all Being, then our souls are emptied of the vibrant force that gives meaning and purpose to our all too bounded time in this world.

The original biblical assertion that *ḥilul Shabbat* is punishable by death is, perhaps needless to say, deeply troubling. The literalism of this Israelite belief was neutralized long ago by the rabbinic inheritors of the biblical tradition, but such language is stunningly dissonant in our postmodern age of voluntarism and individual choice. And yet bold reinterpretation is the engine of creativity within a culture that still wishes to engage with the foundational texts of the tradition. Reimagined through the lens of spiritual metaphor, perhaps the "death" that comes about through a neglect of the Sabbath is a feeling of great distance from the nourishing life-force of holiness. Because the soul gives vitality to the body—an influx of the eternal within the bounded frame of mortal time—the light and vibration of the seventh day have the power to lift our ordinary senses to a new plane of awareness and inspiration, the absence of which may leave us deflated and spiritually lifeless.

For in that he profanes the Sabbath and does not fulfill it
[*mehaleil 'et ha-Shabbat ve-'eino mekaimo*],
the upper life-force—
the supernal Sabbath, which is the aspect of the soul of the world,
withdraws from the world,
and he is like one who has killed the world [*ve-nimtzah horeig 'et ha-'olam*].
For his soul withdraws from him,
and the language of *mehaleil* stems from the language of
ki yimatz'ei halal [if someone slain is found],[11]
which is the language of the taking of a soul [*netilat neshamah*] ... [12]

(continued on page 81)

13 **Our sages taught.** Babylonian Talmud, *Shabbat* 10b.

14 **to draw close to Me.** This statement is framed in the divine first person, as an adaptation of the lines from Tractate *Shabbat*, but it is not itself an actual citation from any source. The Sabbath is a treasure of heavenly origin, bestowed upon the Jewish people as a palpable bridge to the divine Source, and it is through the Sabbath that the people may reconnect to the transcendent realm of God.

15 **His Presence showers onto them.** The drawing down of the Sabbath into this world is identified here with the flowing light of divine emanation; the influx of Shabbat is nothing less than the indwelling of divine presence. As we have seen in other passages, mystics of various religious traditions—and within Judaism in particular—have represented divine Being as a radiant reality, a force of energy that is, at its essence, luminous.[3]

To experience the divine presence is to feel the infusion of supernal light, a vibrant river of otherworldly mystery, an animating wonder that washes through mundane existence, irrigating it with a water born of the hidden spring above. We may also note that the texture of the divine name figures into this portrait of indwelling; Shabbat is experienced in this world as the luminous and dynamic "glorious name." As I discussed above, it is the sacred name of God that often represents the divine Self; the Torah is characterized as the great name of God, and that text functions as a linguistic presence of the deity in this lower world.

[Our sages taught]:[13]
"The Holy One blessed be He said to Moses:
'I have a precious gift hidden in My treasure-house,
and Shabbat is its name.
I wish to give it to the people Israel;
go and make it known to them [*leikh ve-hodi'eim*].'"

The language of *hodi'eim* [make it known to them]
is the language of binding together [*hithabbrut*],
"for through the Sabbath [the people] will attain
a binding and a connection to My light, to My great name—
for without it they would not be able to draw close to Me."[14]
This is so because [finite creatures and infinite Divinity]
are two opposites, as we have discussed above.
But when the supernal Sabbath is drawn down,
when the light of His glorious name
is drawn into this world,
then the people Israel can become attached
to the Creator blessed be He—
to the radiance of His flowing light
that His Presence showers onto them.[15]

(*continued on page 83*)

16 **with Him they become a Oneness.** Here we have a bold and explicit assertion of mystical union, one that clearly reflects the belief among hasidic mystics that the ultimate aim of devotional practice is to achieve a blending of the human self into the all-encompassing whole of Divinity. In its perfect, primordial state, reality is perceived as a single organism of life, all things are elements absorbed into the unity that is divine. Throughout the ages, from Kabbalah to Hasidism, many Jewish mystics averred that the purpose of religious striving was to encounter God with such intensity and love as to become absorbed and reintegrated into Divinity.[4]

The people Israel are characterized as "a divine portion"; they form a part of the larger divine whole, and it is Shabbat that holds the power to bring them back into their primal state of union. Shabbat itself is an indwelling of the divine presence, and so it is Shabbat that binds the people Israel to their divine source.

On the Sabbath we seek to quiet the clamor of ordinary time, to reach inward for a transcendent stillness of mind and soul. For when the rush and noise of the world have been released into tranquility, then we learn to hear the soft music of the earth and its wonders, to intuit the deep unity and integration of this web of life. Shabbat clears the way to a refreshed awareness of the fundamental ways in which we are bound to the root of all living things. Released from the burden of divisions and competition, we return to the grounding rhythm of breath, to the force that gives birth to all speech and song, to all creativity and celebration. It is the radiance of God's flowing light—the *aḥdut* [oneness] that pulses at the center of All.

17 **then they truly become one.** At this moment, all borders and separations are removed; there is no divide between the human being and Divinity. Through the process of cultivated devotion and attachment to the transformative power of the Sabbath, we are opened to receive the influx of divine substance—the oneness of All courses through our soul, and the circle is made complete once again.

[This happens] by virtue of the fact that they are called
a divine portion together with Him [ḥelek YHVH 'immo]—
and with Him they become a Oneness [na'asim 'immo aḥdut] ... [16]

The truth is that when the Creator blessed be He and Israel are united,
[the people] are called one with His blessed name.
For when they are united with Him and attached to Him,
[the divine] portion actually flows and emanates into them
[nishpa' ve-ne'etzal be-tokhan ḥelkav mamash].
When [they are] attached to the All from which flow the [divine]
   elements,
then they truly become one [with God].[17]

Cleansing the Soul
through Washing
and Immersion

Through Your great compassion,
let us merit to have the holiness of the Sabbath
drawn over us
through our washing with hot water
and immersion in the *mikveh*
on the holy Sabbath eve
[on Friday before Shabbat].

Help me, so that I never miss
the washing and the immersion
of the Sabbath eve!

(continued on page 87)

And just as I wash and immerse
myself in this world,
so may You purify and sanctify
my body, my soul, and my spirit
with Your holiness from above—
and may You draw forth the sparks of divine flame
from the holy fire above,
the fire that devours and burns up
all other flames.

And through this fire
I pray that You will burn up
and nullify all the evil
within me and from within
all Your people Israel.

And I pray that the goodness
within us will be sifted
out from that evil,
and that it will ascend high above
to be included in the uppermost Good—
in Your great goodness,
which is the eternal Good.

Likutei Tefilot 1:19

Kiddush

1   **the holiness of Shabbat onto himself.** Holding the cup of wine, reciting the words of the *Kiddush*, we engage in an active process of drawing forth the flow of holiness into the world and onto ourselves. In the moment of ritual we take an essential role in the transformation of time from the ordinary to the sacred. For as we have already seen in the thought of R. Tzadok ha-Kohen, holiness is a cosmic force that requires both divine *and* human action. God infused the core of holiness into Shabbat during the drama of Creation, and still we human beings stimulate and channel the influx of that holiness into our world through our spiritual preparation and ritual behavior. In this passage from Rabbi Natan of Nemirov, chief disciple of Rabbi Naḥman of Bratzlav, the ritual of *Kiddush* is not only a marker of time's transition—a recognition of the Sabbath's entrance—but it is also a process of drawing the cosmic force into our human space. As such, it is a ritual of immense empowerment—an attraction of the divine vitality through our words and our gestures.

Rabbi Natan of Nemirov
Hilkhot Shabbat 6b

The *Kiddush* of the Sabbath eve
is the primary way in which a person draws
the holiness of Shabbat onto himself.[1]

For holiness is wisdom [*ḥokhmah*],
in the sense of *reishit ḥokhmah* [the beginning of wisdom],
and in that every *reishit* is holiness [*kol reishit hu kodesh*].

(continued on page 93)

2   **the dimension of _reishit ḥokhmah_.** As is often the case in Bratzlav hasidic literature, this text is structured according to a series of highly abbreviated and dense associations, each of which carries a rich interpretive and symbolic resonance. The words _ḥokhmah_ (wisdom) and _kodesh_ (holy or holiness) are correlated and identified here through a two-part exegetical association: _reishit_ is identified with _ḥokhmah_ on the basis of a longstanding midrashic tradition that the first word of Genesis (_Bereishit_) should be understood as _be-reishit_: through something called _reishit_, the world was created by God. And what is that _reishit_? It is _ḥokhmah_ (wisdom), on the basis of a reading of Proverbs 8. In that biblical chapter, Lady Wisdom (_ḥokhmah_) speaks aloud, saying (v. 22): "YHVH created me at the beginning of His way" (_YHVH kanani reishit darko_), thus leading the early Rabbis to assert that Wisdom (_ḥokhmah_) was created first and is to be associated with the word _reishit_. The Rabbis of the midrash further claimed that this primordial wisdom is Torah herself in a heavenly, spiritual form—that the world was created through the instrument of Torah.[1]

What is more, in that midrashic text, the word _reishit_ is alternatively interpreted to refer to the people Israel. The second link made by Rabbi Natan of Nemirov in our passage from _Likutei Halakhot_, this time connecting the word _reishit_ to _kodesh_ (holy/holiness), is made via a verse from Jeremiah 2:3: "Israel was holy [_kodesh_] to YHVH, the first [_reishit_] fruits of His harvest [_kodesh Yisra'el le-YHVH, reishit tevuatah_]." The people Israel are here referred to as both _kodesh_ and _reishit_ in a single verse—the perfect interpretive basis for Rabbi Natan's homiletical idea. Thus, in classic midrashic fashion, the hasidic preacher has unified the meanings of the three words (_ḥokhmah_ = _reishit_ = _kodesh_), thereby also deducing that _ḥokhmah_ = _kodesh_ (wisdom = holy/holiness)—the assertion with which he began.

3   **wonders of wisdom [_peli'ot ḥokhmah_].** This terminology is an allusion to the wording of _Sefer Yetzirah_, the ancient work of Jewish esotericism that had a profound effect upon the formation of medieval Kabbalah and later Jewish mysticism. In the anonymously authored _Sefer Yetzirah_, we are told of "thirty-two wondrous paths of wisdom

(continued on page 94)

Through the *Kiddush* [the sanctification]
we ascend to the dimension of *reishit ḥokhmah*—[2]
that is, the root of wisdom in which the wise ones are rooted
[*shoresh ha-ḥokhmah she-ha-ḥakhamim meshurashim sham*]—
the aspect of the wonders of wisdom [*peli'ot ḥokhmah*].[3]

(continued on page 95)

[*netivot peli'ot ḥokhmah*]"—the primal paths of mystery and meaning that were inscribed into the very fabric of Being at the dawn of time. In the ritual of *Kiddush* we are able to ascend to that dimension of wisdom above, that place of wonder within the deepest divine mystery. It is the root of all insight and awareness, a reconnection with the well of Creation—the source of all spiritual consciousness, contained within the thirty-two wondrous paths of wisdom. The words of the *Kiddush* evoke the act of Creation—they are a *zeikher le-ma'aseh bereishit*. And so they return us to that realm before time—to the primordial wisdom through which God created the world, the wisdom that we seek to recapture and absorb on the Sabbath eve.

4   **Wine goes in, and the secret comes out.** Babylonian Talmud, *'Eiruvin* 65a.

5   **they are the wonders of wisdom.** Here the drinking of the Sabbath wine is linked to the attainment of a new state of awareness and mystical consciousness. Just as holiness and wisdom were correlated above, so too the wine of that ritual sanctification is understood to be a part of the transformation of mind that takes place on Shabbat. The statement of the Talmud, *Nikhnas yayin yatza' sod*, "Wine goes in, and the secret comes out," refers to the ability of alcohol to loosen the stops of inhibition; when we drink, we may say things that we otherwise would keep secret. But here the rabbinic saying is given a mystical twist: the ritual drinking of the wine on Friday night is considered to be part of the transformation of consciousness that occurs at the Sabbath table—the secrets of the Torah and primordial wisdom are unlocked through the event of sanctification and the drinking that is integral to that ritual. Our minds are opened in a new way to the life-force of Divinity, the river of holiness that is revealed on Shabbat.[2]

It is for this reason that we sanctify the Sabbath
over a cup of wine—
for the wine of *Kiddush* is the wine of *kedushah* [holiness],
in the sense of:
"Wine goes in, and the secret comes out [*nikhnas yayin yatza 'sod*]!"[4]
Through that wine we attain the secrets of the Torah,
and they are the wonders of wisdom.[5]

This is also the *tikun* [repair/perfection]
of the hands of the angels [*tikun ha-yadayim shel ha-malakhim*],
through which the essence of Sabbath pleasure comes to be.

Therefore, one must hold the cup with both hands.

(*continued on page 97*)

6 **sometimes called *'Elohim.*** This is a very dense set of associations and allusions. In classic interpretive progression, the master first identifies the word *kos* (cup) with the word *'Elohim* (God—or angel, as we shall now see). These two words are found to have the same numerical value to their component letters, and thus the interpreter asserts that they evoke one another by association. That established, Rabbi Natan then invokes the idea, already stated in ancient Jewish interpretation, that in certain cases the divine name *'Elohim* actually refers to an angel and not just to the deity.[3]

On the basis of these correlations, the master then teaches that the cup of wine held during the *Kiddush* alludes to the presence of angels at the Sabbath table, the *malakhim* that escort the Jew into Shabbat. This, after all, is the reason for the recitation of the *Shalom 'Aleikhem* hymn just before *Kiddush*—for it is a song of greeting directed to the heavenly angels who are believed to be present with us at the Sabbath table. What is more, Rabbi Natan (transmitting the wisdom of his teacher, Rabbi Naḥman) understands the moment of *Kiddush* as a repair and perfection of the angelic hands that support our human hands during the ritual act. As we hold the cup of wine, we channel that angelic presence—drawing the heavenly energies into our open palms, directing the spiritual life-force into the wondrous cup of blessing.

Regarding Rabbi Natan's statement that "one must hold the cup with both hands," we should recall that this instruction is already formulated in the Babylonian Talmud (*Berakhot* 51a), though in that classical source the Rabbis explicitly assert that one should take hold of the cup with both hands and then place it in the *right hand*. This rabbinic stipulation is alluded to in the opening page of the *Zohar* (though some scholars have questioned whether this was the original placement of these pages of text),[4] in which the kabbalistic masterwork likens the cup of blessing to a rose among the thorns—a rose with five petals that parallel the five fingers of the human hand. For the *Zohar*, this rose symbolizes the tenth *sefirah*, *Shekhinah*, and the person is instructed to hold the *Kiddush* cup in one hand ("on five

(*continued on page 98*)

For the word "cup" [*kos*] is the numerical equivalent [*gematria*]
of the word *'Elohim*—
in the sense of the word "angel" [*malakh*],
which is sometimes called *'Elohim*.[6]
One must hold the cup with both hands in the moment of *Kiddush*
because it is through the *Kiddush* that the hands are perfected
[*ki 'al yedei ha-kiddush nittaknim ha-yadayim*]—
the power of the hands is returned to the angel.

This is further reflected in the seventy words of the *Kiddush*,
which correspond to the seventy faces of the Torah.

For through the faith of the wise,
which a person draws onto himself through the *Kiddush*,
and through which one attains the essence of Sabbath pleasure
[*'ikar 'oneg Shabbat*]—
through this we attain the seventy faces of Torah.

(continued on page 99)

fingers, and no more"). Though the right hand is not mentioned explicitly in this zoharic passage, we may assume this to be the intention, given both the talmudic basis and the kabbalistic belief that the *Shekhinah*, who represents the lower *middat ha-din* (force of judgment) and is symbolized by the left hand, must be enveloped and contained within *Ḥesed* (the force of compassion), symbolized by the right hand. Thus, in the view of the *Zohar*, by holding the *Kiddush* cup in our right hand we send the blessing of compassion and *Ḥesed* into the fragile and sacred *Shekhinah*.

7   **seventy faces of Torah.** Here the transformation of consciousness on Friday night is textured even further. The *Kiddush* itself is compared to the Torah and the fullness of its potential meanings. The midrashic Sages used the expression "seventy faces of the Torah" to evoke the seemingly uncountable, and perhaps infinite, number of interpretations that can be discovered in the Torah (see *Midrash Bemidbar Rabbah* 13:15). It is a well of eternally renewed meanings, reverberating through the generations with the unceasing voice of divine revelation. The ritual of *Kiddush*, which Rabbi Natan has already correlated to the discovery of new spiritual wisdom and awareness, is here framed as a resonance of the eternal voice of Sinai—the seventy words that compose the liturgical text of the *Kiddush* over wine embody the uncontainable array of meanings that flow forth from the spring of Torah.

Rabbi Natan does, however, enfold this font of wisdom within the persona of the wise one—the great mystical sage who transmits the spiritual depths to his disciples and community. Here Rabbi Natan reveals the degree to which truth was thought to be mediated through a charismatic and revered sage. The hasidic master was often understood by his disciples (and this attitude was on prominent display in Bratzlav Hasidism) to be the conduit between heaven and earth, the pillar through which divine light and wisdom are transmitted to the earthly realm.

For all seventy faces of Torah are drawn forth
through the faith of the wise—
they interpret the Torah for us,
and they preach its meanings in seventy ways.
And without the wise ones
we could not know any of the faces of Torah.
For we do not know any interpretation, clarification, or meaning of the
    Torah
except through the faith of the wise.

Thus it is through the *Kiddush*—
the time when we ascend to the wonders of wisdom
and draw forth the faith of the wise—
it is through this that we draw forth the holiness
of the seventy faces of Torah.[7]

An Intention for Eating
on the Sabbath

Through Your great compassion
let me merit to receive the Sabbath in a fitting manner:
with joy, abundance, and honor—
and with a diminishment of sin.

Let me be strengthened with all my might
to partake of an array of delicacies, foods, and drinks
in honor of the holy Sabbath.

For Sabbath eating is all Divinity, all holiness—
and it ascends to an entirely different place
than does eating during the workweek.

Let me merit, through holy Sabbath eating,
to repair the flaw of Sabbath desecration.

Only You can guard and save me from
all the kinds of Sabbath desecration
that exist in the world!

(continued on page 103)

Help me merit to have abundance
in Sabbath eating
until, through this, I am able to repair
every flaw of Sabbath desecration
that I have incurred.

Help me to receive the Sabbath
with great holiness and joy,
and to have abundance in the Sabbath meal.

And through this holy Sabbath eating,
let me merit to expand and to magnify
all the holy and true paths that we must travel
in order to draw closer to You in truth.

Likutei Tefilot 1:107

Eating and Contemplation

1 **Torah of the Ancient One.** In these brief lines, Rabbi Natan of Nemirov has alluded to several complicated ideas. The highest form of mystical knowledge in Bratzlav hasidic thought, the contemplation of the innermost mysteries of Divinity, is called *'Oraita' de-'Atika'* (the Torah/teaching of *'Atik*/the Ancient of Days). This corresponds to the highest *sefirah* in the medieval Kabbalah of the *Zohar*, in which the phrase *'Atik Yomin*, "Ancient of Days," refers to the *sefirah Keter* (Crown). Already in the *Zohar*, and developed in new ways by Rabbi Isaac Luria in sixteenth-century Tzfat, the *sefirah* known as *'Atik Yomin* was believed to contain the most recondite and mysterious secrets of divine reality—for these kabbalists, and for the Bratzlav mystics as well, this secret knowledge was associated with the revelations reserved for the messianic era. To know God is to uncover the mysteries of the *sefirot*, and to know the highest of these divine dimensions is to enable a messianic consciousness. This elevated state of mind is here called *hitbonenut*, a mode of awareness that transforms the person's perception of Being and cosmic truth. The Sabbath is the time in which the human mind is opened to the depths of divine reality; spiritual consciousness reaches a transcendent state of knowing.

2 **attained on Shabbat.** Here the allusion is made to the passages from the *Zohar* that kabbalists and hasidim recite prior to the start of each of the three holy meals of the Sabbath (Friday night dinner, Saturday lunch, Saturday late afternoon/evening meal), a custom that was first established by Isaac Luria in sixteenth-century Tzfat. The first of these passages, recited on Friday evening, refers to the delight (*'oneg*) that is stimulated in the highest *sefirah* (*Keter*/*'Atika' Kadisha'*/*'Atik*) through the delight and pleasure (*'oneg*) of the Jewish people on the Sabbath.

3 *yarei' Shabbat.* One of the ways that Jewish interpreters have played with the word *Bereishit* (in the beginning) is to break apart the word and rearrange its letters to form the two words ירא שבת (*yarei' Shabbat*), a phrase that evokes both awe of the Sabbath and extreme care in fulfilling its ritual details. Utilizing this interpretive play, Rabbi Natan teaches that the awe and fear of heaven that is particularly strong

(continued on page 108)

Likutei Halakhot

Rabbi Natan of Nemirov
Hilkhot Shabbat 1

On Shabbat we attain
the state of contemplative knowing [*hitbonenut*],
and this is *'Oraita' de-'Atika'*,
the Torah of the Ancient One,[1]
the aspect of "seek the delight of God" [*tit'aneig 'al YHVH*]
that is attained on Shabbat.[2]

For Shabbat is the aspect of *yir'ah* [fear/awe],
the aspect of *yarei' Shabbat* [being in awe of Shabbat].
And this is *Bereishit—yarei' Shabbat*.[3]

(continued on page 109)

on Shabbat is hinted at in the first word of the Torah: *Bereishit*. And both are associated with the first *sefirah*, called the Holy Ancient One (*'Atika' Kadisha'*).

4 **the divine Torah.** When referring to the Torah of *'Atika' Kadisha'*, Rabbi Natan is clearly alluding to *Keter*, the first *sefirah*, but the notion stated here—that *Bereishit* hints at the upper divine Torah—is a reference to the kabbalistic parsing of the word *Bereishit* as *be-reishit*, through the *sefirah* Ḥokhmah, also known as the upper preexistent Torah within the divine self. As mentioned earlier, this interpretive move was modeled on the commentary already expressed in *Midrash Bereishit Rabbah* of the ancient Rabbis, in which the word *reishit* was correlated to the word *ḥokhmah* (wisdom) on the basis of the usage in Proverbs 8 (see my discussion of this in the chapter titled "*Kiddush*").

✦ To sum up this complicated series of associations: Shabbat contains within it the mystery of a divine wisdom that predates the creation of the world (Shabbat is correlated to this meaning of the word *Bereishit* through the equation of the words ירא שבת to בראשית, forms that contain the same letters). For this reason, on Shabbat Jews are able to access the upper Torah, held within the *sefirah* called *'Atika' Kadisha'* (the Holy Ancient One). This is especially so during the Friday evening meal, the time when the mystics believe Jews are most open to that deepest mystery of divine existence. As we will continue to observe, both Rabbi Natan and his teacher Rabbi Naḥman employ a strikingly associative method of mystical interpretation. Ideas and words are linked together in a web of associations through the connector term *beḥinah* (aspect or dimension), thereby fashioning a weave of meaning and interpretive value.

5 **an unbounded inheritance.** Babylonian Talmud, *Shabbat* 118a.

For *Bereishit* is the aspect of the upper Torah,
the divine Torah.[4]

Thus, through Shabbat we attain
a great richness [*'al yedei Shabbat zokhin le-'ashirut gadol*],
as our Rabbis of blessed memory said:
"Everyone who takes pleasure on Shabbat
attains an unbounded inheritance [*nahalah beli meitzarim*]."[5]

The essence depends precisely upon
the pleasure of Shabbat [*ve-'ikar talui be-'oneg Shabbat davka'*],
and this pleasure is found in the act of eating on the Sabbath.

(continued on page 111)

6   **we attain the Face.** Here the allusion is to the illumined divine face, a mystical image used extensively in the medieval Kabbalah of the *Zohar* and the sixteenth-century Kabbalah of Isaac Luria.

7   **illuminates his face.** Ecclesiastes 8:1.

8   **through Sabbath eating.** In these lines Rabbi Natan has offered a bold and surprising teaching. The transformed state of mind that comes about on the Sabbath is directly connected to the physical pleasures of the holy day. The act of eating on Shabbat is understood to be a spiritual moment through which a new consciousness, a new wisdom, is attained. We experience the illumined face of contemplative knowing—a reflection of the upper shining face of Divinity—in the pleasure of Sabbath sleep, a state that is brought about through the pleasure of eating the Sabbath meals. How many of us have savored that special pleasure of the Sabbath, the rest that follows a satisfying meal?

What we see here, however, is a framing of that eating and resting, those delicious pleasures of the day, as elements of spiritual practice. These are not just physical pleasures for their own sake: through pleasure the Jew arrives at a new level of spiritual wisdom and awareness; pleasure is the channel for the attainment of contemplative knowing. This is quite the opposite of an ascetic practice, a path in which physical pleasure is avoided and subjugated for the sake of a perceived higher spiritual good. Here the pleasures of the body are embraced as integral parts of an elevated spiritual practice!

As I discussed above, the Sabbath meals were understood by the kabbalists and the hasidim to be times of sacred alignment with the inner dimensions of God—the Friday night meal directed to the highest *sefirah*, and so on. Recalling the opening of our commentary to this Bratzlav teaching, the first meal of the Sabbath—the eating that follows the Friday night *Kiddush*—is intended toward *'Atika' Kadisha'* (the Holy Ancient One), the dimension of Divinity that contains the deepest mysteries of wisdom and Torah. The eating that takes place in the context of the sacred ritual meal leads the Jew toward a contemplative knowing (*hitbonenut*) of that upper wisdom—that exalted part of God.

(continued on page 112)

For Sabbath eating is the arousal of sleep:
through Sabbath eating we attain the Face,[6]
the aspect of "the wisdom of a man illuminates his face
[ḥokhmat 'adam ta'ir panav],"[7]
the aspect of the shining face ['anpin nehirin] that we attain
precisely through Sabbath eating.[8]

For Rabbi Natan—consciously transmitting the teachings of his master, Rabbi Naḥman—the Sabbath is a time of contemplative transformation, an experience in which spiritual awareness is opened and elevated to new heights of mystical understanding. And this happens through a mindful practice of eating during the holy meal, as well as in the sleep that follows.

Rabbi Natan's teaching may be adapted as a *kavvanah* (an intention) for mindful eating, and the way in which we approach the ritual process of the Sabbath meals may guide us into a mind transformed, a consciousness of the divine mystery and sacred purpose that pervades this time of wonder and restoration. As Rabbi Natan emphasizes at the beginning of the teaching, Shabbat is a time when we know differently, a realm of experience in which our spiritual awareness is lifted beyond the turmoil of ordinary workday pressures, elevated to a recharged sense of the divine center in our lives. Implicit in the master's words is the idea that the pleasures of Shabbat are fundamentally different from the pleasures of ordinary time; our experience of eating on the Sabbath dwells on a higher spiritual plane than our practice of eating in ordinary moments during the week.

We might think of this along the lines suggested by the philosopher Leon Kass in his book *The Hungry Soul*, when eating is transformed from basic animal sustenance to the nobility of human dining, it cultivates the friendship and fellowship on which we build the purpose and beauty of our humanity.[1] And in our case, eating on the Sabbath becomes a moment of deep mindfulness in which the meal is aligned with its divine anchor. By entering into the sacred meal with this intention, our consciousness is opened to the great divine purpose of our lives in this world, the cycle of ordinary and holy time. In the Sabbath we discover a spiritual force that is at once ancient and yet-to-come—the space in which the perfection of old touches the redemption of the world to come, the circle of time revealed to be but one and inseparable.

Let us allow the time of Sabbath eating—meals aglow with the light of candles and the soul fellowship of family and friends—to become a time of deep spiritual attunement to the mystery and wonder of our lives. Let us become mindful of the way in which the divine force of energy fills this moment, making it whole and bringing us to a new awareness of the spiritual purpose that fills our comings and goings all week long.

Transforming Our Speech

Help us to sanctify our mouths
and our speech on the Sabbath day,
that our speech on Shabbat
not be like our speech during
the ordinary days of the week.

Master of the world,
have compassion for us,
and sanctify us through all
of the kinds of holiness
that are part of the holy Sabbath—
with joy and great delight,
with awe and love—
until we merit to be absorbed
into the sanctity of the holy Sabbath,
and to draw that holiness
onto the six days of the week.

Likutei Tefilot 1:31

Ḥallah as a Symbol
of Spiritual Wholeness

1   **all the evildoers are scattered.** Psalm 92:10. This psalm is also included in the Friday night liturgy.

2   **the Other Side.** This Aramaic phrase is drawn from the *Zohar*, where it connotes the demonic evil dimension of the upper realm. The root of all evil in the lower world, the Other Side (*Sitra' 'Aḥra'*) derives its power as a force mutated from the divine aspect of justice and severity. Many medieval Jews believed that all week long the demonic forces of the Other Side lurk in the shadows, waiting to cause harm and pollution to Jews seeking to do God's will. But on Shabbat, the forces of good and light overpower and banish the forces of evil darkness—Jews and the *Shekhinah* are able to dwell in peace. Rabbi Natan's formulation here echoes this older notion, asserting that these forces of darkness hold no sway over the domain of holiness on the Sabbath. The demonic Other Side is also likened to the filthy clothing of ordinary time, a garb that is stripped away in preparation for the cleansing and fresh garb of Shabbat. In these lines, Rabbi Natan underscores that the Sabbath meal constitutes one of the great heights of such holiness and purity—a time when (as we saw in our previous Bratzlav text) access to Divinity is enabled, liberated from the obstructions and pollution of profane time.

3   **filthy garments.** Zechariah 3:3.

Likutei Halakhot

Rabbi Natan of Nemirov
Hilkhot Se'udah 5:9

Shabbat is a semblance of the world to come,
and it is a great *mitzvah* to eat then;
it is the essence of honoring the Sabbath.

For on Shabbat "all the evildoers are scattered [*yitpardu kol po'alei 'aven*],"[1]
and the Other Side [*Sitra' 'Aḥra'*][2]—
which is the aspect of "filthy garments [*begadim tzo'im*]"[3]—
has no hold or draw on the food of Shabbat.

(continued on page 119)

4　**garments clean and white.** We observed similar formulations in the chapter "Wearing White on Shabbat." It should be noted, however, that the present text (from the pen of Rabbi Natan) is much older than the one authored by R. Tzadok ha-Kohen of Lublin. The process of washing for the Sabbath, as well as the ritual immersion in the *mikveh* bath, is again understood as a purification of both body and spirit—they are practices that embody the stripping away of the Other Side, the uncovering of the soul, and an entrance into the eternal dimension of Shabbat—referred to here (as before) as a semblance of the transcendent world to come.

5　***beirur* is achieved.** Here we have our first mention of a core theme in this passage: the Lurianic kabbalistic notion of *beirur*—the sifting and excavation of the divine sparks hidden in the coarse and material world. According to that sixteenth-century mythology, the first stage of creation involved the channeling of a primordial divine light into vessels. But the force of infinity present in that light proved too powerful for the vessels, and they shattered, sending shards of broken vessels falling into what would become our lower physical world. And all of those shards contain fallen sparks that must ultimately be raised back up to their infinite source for true cosmic redemption to be achieved. *Beirur* is thus the very human work of excavating those sparks beneath the surface of mundane reality, primarily through the performance of *mitzvot* with the proper intentionality.[1]

This drama was particularly appealing to later hasidic mystical thinkers, for whom *beirur* became a spiritual practice of attention and discovery. All around us lie the sparks of fallen light, and we must cultivate a mind focused on such a quest—a mode of daily perception in which every aspect of our ordinary existence holds the potential for a hidden ray of Divinity. The sacred dwells in unexpected places, and so we must live our religious lives as a kind of contemplative sifting and clarification—we must excavate the very earth of ourselves, we must break through the outer layers of accumulated dust and time to uncover the primal presence of the Divine, the light inherent since the birth of physical reality. A day that holds the power of redemption and perfection, a

(continued on page 120)

For Sabbath eating is entirely holy [*ki 'akhilat Shabbat kulo kodesh*].
This is the aspect of washing with hot water [*rehitzat hamin*]
and immersion [in the *mikveh*] on the Sabbath eve [before Shabbat].
After this, a person dresses in holy Sabbath clothes—
for the people cleanse themselves
of the aspect of "filthy garments [*begadim tzo'im*],"
and afterward they dress in Sabbath clothes,
garments clean and white.[4]

[They do this] because Shabbat is a semblance of the world to come,
a time when the ultimate completion [and perfection]
of *beirur* is achieved[5]
in the sense of holy eating,

(*continued on page 121*)

glimpse of the world to come, the Sabbath is "a time when the ultimate completion [and perfection] of *beirur* is achieved." The divine sparks that lie hidden in mundane reality all through the six days of ordinary time are revealed and elevated on the day that is all soul. For just as the process of uncovering those fallen sparks and elevating them back to their cosmic origin is integral to the kabbalistic drama of redemption, so too the redemptive character of Shabbat is marked by its ability to bring the sparks to completion and perfection. On the Sabbath, we are blessed with the wonder of clear perception; the sacred force of the day opens our eyes to a new kind of spiritual awareness and attention. This is the *beirur*—the excavation—that is attained on the seventh day. For it is both an excavation and a clarification of the contemplative mind; on Shabbat we rise to a heavenly condition of revelation and understanding. We see the divine lights in a new way: hidden during the workweek, they are opened to us within the passageways of holy time.

In this paradigm, the future redemption is understood to constitute a *restoration* of the primordial and original state of cosmic perfection. The end-time is linked back to the time of origins, thereby creating a unified temporal arc.[2]

6 **let the lowly eat and be satisfied.** Psalm 22:27.

7 ***leḥem mishneh* on Shabbat.** The *leḥem mishneh* is already mentioned in the Torah (Exodus 16:22) in reference to the double portion of bread that the wandering Israelites were commanded to collect on the sixth day of the week to prepare for the coming Sabbath. This biblical source shaped a fundamental structure of Sabbath ritual and eating practices in the history of Judaism, one in which two whole (unbroken) loaves of bread are used at the Friday night meal to signify the practice of collecting and preparing food for the Sabbath day on Friday. See, for example, Babylonian Talmud, *Shabbat* 117b. Also see Rabbi Yaakov ben 'Asher (d. ca. 1340), *'Arba' Turim, 'Oraḥ Ḥayyim* 274; and Rabbi Yosef Karo (d. 1575), *Shulḥan 'Arukh, 'Oraḥ Ḥayyim* 274:1–4.

in the sense of "let the lowly eat and be satisfied
[yo'khlu 'anavim ve-yisba'u]."[6]

This is how we should understand the meaning of
leḥem mishneh [the double portion of bread] on Shabbat,[7]
for all the excavations [beirurim] that are made
during ḥol [non-sacred time] through the labors that pertain,
for the most part, to matters of bread—

(continued on page 123)

8 **all of these are nullified on Shabbat.** All the labors and actions that we engage in during the workweek are also behaviors that endeavor to uncover the sparks hidden in the mundane realm. Several of the halakhic categories of labor forbidden on Shabbat are actions associated with the farming procedures necessary to make bread—planting, plowing, and harvesting—and thus the sacred bread of Shabbat is understood to represent the ultimate completion and redemption of these activities. In the wholeness of the *ḥallah*, all the work that was needed to bring the loaf into being is raised up to a spiritual plane; all of the divine sparks that were excavated through the different labors of harvesting are unified in the *ḥallah*, and they are brought to redemption through the sacred act of blessing and eating.

9 *yarei' Shabbat.* This play on words, in which the word *bereishit* (בראשית) is understood to contain the phrase *yarei' Shabbat* (ירא שבת)—in the sense of the reverential and pious practice of the Sabbath—was discussed in my commentary to the preceding text selected from Rabbi Natan's *Likutei Halakhot* ("Eating and Contemplation").

10 **all six days are blessed.** This phrase and idea, which is drawn from the *Zohar* (2:63b, 2:88a), represents the Sabbath as a wellspring of spiritual energy, a fountain from which flows the life and animation of the other six days of the week. As we saw earlier in R. Tzadok ha-Kohen's adaptation, this construction understands Shabbat as the source of nourishment for the rest of the week in a manner that parallels the way that the six "middle *sefirot*" within Divinity (*Ḥesed, Gevurah, Tif'eret, Netzaḥ, Hod, Yesod*) receive the flux of emanation from the *sefirah Binah*—referred to, along with the *sefirah Shekhinah*, as the Shabbat within the divine realm.

including planting [*zorei'a*], plowing [*horeish*], and harvesting [*kotzeir*]—
all of these are nullified on Shabbat.[8]

For on Shabbat there is no *beirur;*
all the *beirurim* of the six days of the week ascend to their rest,
and they are completed and perfected on Shabbat with ultimate
    perfection,
which is *yir'ah* [fear/awe],
in the sense of *bereishit* [בראשית]—*yarei' Shabbat* [ירא שבת].[9]

Even the power to make those excavations during *hol*
comes from the holiness of Shabbat,
which is drawn forth into the six days of the week;
for from [the Sabbath] all six days are blessed
[*mitbarkha'an kol shita' yomin*].[10]

It is for this reason that we assemble *lehem mishneh* on Shabbat—
two whole loaves of bread [*shnei lehamim sheleimim*].
For during *hol*, even though a person should strive to
[say the blessing] over a complete bread loaf,
it is not obligatory....

(*continued on page 125*)

11   **the essence of the rest and cessation of Shabbat.** *Menuḥah* is a cosmic force: not only does a *person* rest on the Sabbath, but the scattered lights of Divinity seek out their rest on the seventh day as well. This is also a play on the word *Shabbat*: as numerous Jewish interpreters have observed through the ages, the Hebrew word שבת (*shavat*) contains another Hebrew word—שב (*shav*), or לשוב (*lashuv*)—return. The Sabbath is a time of personal and cosmic returning—a coming back to the source of all vitality and spiritual renewal. Several thinkers have understood this to teach that Shabbat is the ultimate enabler of תשובה (*teshuvah*, literally "return," but also the classic Hebrew word for repentance). See the formulation in *Sefer Ḥemdat Yamim, 'Aseret Yemei Teshuvah,* 6. For a classic hasidic homily on the correlation between שבת (*Shabbat/shavat*) and השבה (*hashavah*), see Rabbi Meshullam Feibush Heller of Zbarazh, *Yosher Divrei 'Emet,* 46. In our text at hand from the Bratzlav school, this theme of return on Shabbat is extended to the sparks that have been uncovered and excavated during the week through a discipline of spiritual focus and intentionality; the Sabbath is not a time of further excavation—for such questing is understood to be a form of labor reserved for the workweek—it is instead a time of return and tranquility, the day when all the cosmos reaches a state of pure stillness and repose.

12   **an initial cut into the *leḥem mishneh*.** According to the Ba'al ha-Turim (as Rabbi Yaakov ben 'Asher is often called), many Jews rejected this practice, based on the understanding that the *mitzvah* of *leḥem mishneh* requires whole loaves. See the comments in R. Yaakov ben 'Asher, *'Arba' Turim, 'Oraḥ Ḥayyim,* 167.

On Shabbat, all the sparks that have been excavated [*she-nitbareru*]
during all the days of *ḥol*
immediately ascend to their place of rest—
for this is the essence of the rest and cessation of Shabbat
[*she-zehu 'ikar ha-menuḥah ve-ha-shevitah shel Shabbat*].[11]

For this reason do we make [an initial] cut
into the *leḥem mishneh* [before fully slicing the loaf],[12]
in order to indicate that even at the approaching moment of actual
   slicing
the wholeness and perfection is not nullified,
for the second whole loaf is still set [uncut] upon the table.

(continued on page 127)

13 **whole and complete.** As we have seen, the requirement of having two unbroken loaves on the table is a halakhic stipulation that was developed within the Jewish legal tradition. But what we see here is an effort to imbue a legal structure with spiritual and mystical meaning. The loaves of *hallah* that we place on the Sabbath table must be whole precisely because they signify the state of wholeness and redemptive perfection that is manifest on Shabbat. All week long we toil in the marketplace of division and brokenness; we encounter a society that is all too often pervaded by greed and ego, by vanity and selfishness. We wander about in search of the divine unity that lies within all Being; we yearn for a reconnection to the essence and ground of life—a liberation from superficiality. Shabbat comes as a revelation of that *sheleimut*, a glimpse of what it is to become *shaleim*, to become whole and complete in our spiritual and physical lives. For just as the Sabbath candlelight alludes to the divine radiance that dwells as an eternal soul in the center of Being, so too the wholeness of the *hallah* can lead us to a new awareness of the reunification of all that lies broken in ourselves—in our relationships with other people, in our quest for authenticity and honesty, in our engagement with our community and our society. The wholeness of the *hallah* symbolizes the integration and the bonded synergy that we seek between the diverse strands of our lives; it calls us to a renewed self-examination, cultivating an attunement to the unified rhythm and melody that flows beneath the surface.

Now, on Shabbat, the quality of wholeness is not nullified
from the table [*'ein nitbateil behinat ha-sheleimut mei-ha-shulhan*],
not even at the moment of full slicing.
For at that time of slicing, the life-force inherent in the bread
ascends to the ultimate height of its wholeness
[*'oleh ha-hiyut she-ba-lehem le-takhlit sheleimuto*].
And this is the meaning of *lehem mishneh*:
even at the moment of cutting
the second loaf remains whole and complete.[13]

(*continued on page 129*)

14   **the shelter of peace that is spread over us on the Sabbath.** This reference to the "shelter of peace" is an allusion to the liturgy of the Sabbath eve in which the distinctive wording of the *Hashkiveinu* prayer is notably different from the wording of the *Hashkiveinu* for weekday evenings. In both the Shabbat version and the weekday version, the first part of the prayer includes the words *u-fros 'aleinu sukkat shelomekha* ("Spread over us the shelter of Your peace")—an expression that takes the form of a petition, beseeching God for the gift of divine peace, spiritual shelter. In the Shabbat version, however, the *Hashkiveinu* prayer includes the motif two additional times—the second of the three instances in the same petitionary form as the first (*u-fros 'aleinu sukkat shelomekha*), and the third (offered in the closing line of the prayer) in the form of *recognition* as opposed to petition (*ha-pores sukkat shalom 'aleinu*—"Blessed are You, *YHVH*, who spreads the shelter of peace over us"). Why the different form that implies a peace that has already been granted by God to the world? This, we might suggest, is exactly the point: on Shabbat, unlike during the six days of the week, that divine shelter of peace has already come to dwell in the world. The consciousness of weekday time is that of a prayer for deliverance from the chaos and dissonance of the physical; on Shabbat we are able to recognize that God has now bestowed the gift of peace—we now dwell in the wonder of redemption.

And what is true *shalom*, true peace? It is the *sheleimut* of the world, wholeness and redemption. It is the shelter of divine indwelling, the space within which we intuit the interconnected unity of God, nature, and person. People suffer in our home cities and in distant regions of the world. And though the pain of poverty and the scourge of injustice do not disappear with the lighting of the Sabbath candles, Shabbat does open up a vision of a world redeemed; we taste the dream of an earth blessed with perfection, an ideal that we can work toward again with renewed strength in the week to come. The wholeness and illumination of Shabbat call us to raise up the brokenness of this world and all who are driven low by its pain. Like the *mitzvah* to say the blessing over *ḥallot* that are

(*continued on page 130*)

For on Shabbat, the essence of *shalom* [peace]
is the aspect of *sheleimut* [wholeness and completion],
in the sense of the shelter of peace [*sukkat shalom*]
that is spread over us on the Sabbath.[14]

whole, we are commanded to seek out the sparks that have been scattered and exiled—to make them whole again. The *leḥem mishneh* is a reminder to us that Shabbat is a glimpse of a world restored and perfected, but it must also awaken us to the holy work of lifting up our fellow human beings from where they have fallen.

Reading the Torah Portion as a Spiritual Practice

May it be Your will that I take pains to fulfill
all the needs of the Sabbath on my own,
with great strength and diligence.

Help me to always complete
the entire Torah portion with the community—
that we may be blessed to read the portion of the week every
Sabbath eve,
twice in the language of Scripture and once in translation—
with great concentration, with holiness and with purity—
that through this we may achieve
the perfection of the holy language [of Hebrew]
through the language of translation.

Likutei Tefilot 1:19

Refraining from Labor

1 **to have the soul overpower the body.** As we have seen in the thought of other hasidic masters, the days of the workweek are likened to the limited and all too physical character of this world. The Sabbath, however, is understood to be a portal into the realm of pure spirit and soul—it is there that we touch the terrain of redemption. Here the thirty-nine kinds of labor that are forbidden on Shabbat are correlated to that physical character of the six days. We must nullify and transcend those labors on Shabbat precisely because they represent the life of the body. All week long we work in the deeply corporeal texture of ordinary being; we are caught up in the toil of physical sustenance and existence. But on the Sabbath we are granted a reprieve from our daily focus on the body and its needs. On the Sabbath, we reach beyond the limits of our palpable mortality and the weight of materiality; we are liberated for a time from an enslaved consciousness.

Yom Kippur, several hasidic mystics teach us, is called *Shabbat Shabbaton*—a Sabbath of Sabbaths—because on that holiest day we come the closest that we can to experiencing the world to come, the time when we truly transcend the body. As the tradition asserts (Babylonian Talmud, *Kallah* 2), in the world to come there is no eating and no drinking; through fasting and the other abstentions of Yom Kippur, we reach for a moment beyond the bounds of mortal consciousness, we touch a place that transcends physicality and finitude. If Shabbat is *mei-'ein 'olam ha-ba'*—a semblance of the world to come—then Yom Kippur takes us even closer. Like the Day of Atonement, our weekly experience of Shabbat holds the power to lift us beyond the mundane constraints of our ordinary physical existence. It enables us to become better attuned to the nuances of spirit and soul.

And yet, ironically, Shabbat is hardly the model of true physical abstention that Yom Kippur may be. For at the heart of Sabbath life is festivity and celebration. On Shabbat, we rejoice in eating, resting, sex, and fellowship. We savor delight (*'oneg*), not suffering! So how are we to understand this transcendence of the physical on the Sabbath? In what ways do we strive for the triumph of the soul over the body? In order to reach that place of joy and festivity, we must transform our ordinary weekday approach to physical gratification and

(*continued on page 136*)

Likutei Halakhot

Rabbi Natan of Nemirov
Hilkhot Ḥodesh 3:9

The essence of nullifying labor on Shabbat—
all 39 labors (ל"ט מלאכות)—
is so that one may merit to have the soul overpower the body
[*bishvil lizkot lehagbir ha-nefesh 'al ha-guf*];[1]

(*continued on page 137*)

materiality. Shabbat does involve a significant withdrawal from the mundane world around us. We "unplug" from the constant stream of digital media that pervades our seeing and hearing in ordinary time; we step back from writing and earning and cooking. We return ourselves to the quiet simplicity of life, to a place where the stillness of mind can observe holiness where it was once obscured, where we can once again hear the mysterious sound of silence—the divine *kol demamah dakah*.

2   **the dew of lights.** Here the Hebrew letters ל"ט, which stand numerically for the thirty-nine forms of labor that are forbidden on Shabbat, are inverted to yield the Hebrew word *tal,* טל, which means "dew." When the thirty-nine labors are nullified into the pure spirituality of the Sabbath day, when we are able to rise above the physicality and materiality of work, then we are blessed with the flow of divine radiance—the "dew of lights," the *tal 'orot,* טל אורות. We invert the ל"ט into ט"ל—our enslavement to corporeality and labor is transformed into the ethereal light of Divinity, we stand in the presence of an otherworldly glow. This radiance only emerges once we have left the world of work behind us; we receive a revelation of the world to come, that glimpse only visible on Shabbat.

This inversion of the Hebrew letters signifies an inversion of our ordinary selves. We need to turn ourselves inside out, to completely upend the way we are during workaday time. The ל"ט of the *melakhot* (the labors) represents our bodily selves; the טל אורות represents our spiritual selves, a heavenly glow that shines outward from the depths of the soul. On Shabbat we merit to attain an elevated and opened consciousness; ours is a mind and a perception washed through and revived by the "dew of lights." For it is also the "dew of rejuvenation," the *tal shel teḥiyah,* and "eternal life" (*ḥayyim nitzḥiyim*). Shabbat holds the force of the eternal in its heart, a dynamic that Abraham Joshua Heschel characterized as "eternity utters a day" in his classic and inspirational work on the meaning of the Sabbath in modern times.[1] Shabbat is the bridge between the finite, mortal realm and the infinite, eternal dimension of existence. Bound to the life-flow of Divinity, Shabbat draws from the well of unbounded energy,

(*continued on page 138*)

that we may merit the dew of lights [*tal 'orot*—ט"ל אורות],[2]
the dew of rejuvenation [*tal shel teḥiyah*],

(*continued on page 139*)

from the fountain of all Being. But what indeed does it mean for Shabbat to embody the *ḥayyim nitzḥiyim*, eternal life? In what way is the Sabbath a portal to eternity, an indwelling of the everlasting? The *raza' de-Shabbat*, the mystery of the Sabbath, unites us with the many generations that have gone before us. We can envision the countless lives that have been sheltered and uplifted by its holiness and gentle beauty. It cuts through the borders of deep time. But there is also something at once primordial and transcendent about this inner courtyard of the divine temple. In our moments of greatest tranquility, we hear and feel the soft vibrations of divine presence, hidden beneath the surface, and still always there. Shabbat appears in time, and yet it touches the timeless—the world to come, which is all Sabbath (*yom she-kulo Shabbat*).

We must nullify and invert our normal selves in order to reach this mysterious terrain. Through preparation for holiness, we reach deep into the darkness of infinity—the dimension where the Nothing gives birth to the known, where the edges of the mind are found and lost again. Crossing the boundaries between *ḥol* and *kodesh*, between the ordinary and the sacred, we transfigure ל"ט consciousness—our obsession with the mundane and the material—into ט"ל consciousness, an awareness fresh as dew, renewing our perception as completely as the *teḥiyat ha-meitim* (the resurrection of the dead). Indeed, mundane and superficial awareness may here be understood as a kind of spiritual death, a lifelessness from which we seek revival. Entrance into the holy, transcendence of our enslavement to physicality: that is liberation from a deadened soul, absorption of the eternity that dwells within the Sabbath.

3   **merit eternal life.** From the liturgy of the Sabbath *Musaf* service.

eternal life [*ḥayyim nitzḥiyim*], in the sense of
"those who taste [of the Sabbath] merit eternal life"
[*to'ameḥa ḥayyim zakhu*].[3]

(continued on page 141)

4   **that we recite on Shabbat.** Found in the liturgical segment of the *Shaḥarit* service that begins with the words *ha-kol yodukha*. This section directly follows the *Barkhu* prayer. Transmitting the thought of Rabbi Naḥman, Rabbi Natan here teaches that our recitation of these lines in the Sabbath liturgy signals the spiritual transformation that takes place on the seventh day. We are, as expressed in the previous note, elevated to a different plane of living on the Sabbath. It is a kind of rebirth, an entry into life resurrected from the deadened dross of superficial consciousness. There is an awakening to eternity and new vitality that occurs on Shabbat. The Friday night air whispers with the sweetness of redemption and a soul reborn.

5   **their souls overpower their bodies.** In this powerful statement, the master attributes our general human tendency to discord (*maḥloket*) to our inability to transcend the physical. When we are dominated by mundane consciousness, when we have not cultivated an inner eye of spiritual sight and perception, we are often trapped in an endless cycle of competition and conflict, imprisoned by our own desires and instincts. We must reach beyond this state of mind to the more rarefied and sublime rhythm of the soul. When we have aligned our awareness to the vibrations of the spirit, when we have become attuned to the mystery that breathes at the center of all Being, then all the petty divisions of this world will be left behind and outgrown. We will then be able to see matters in their depth, the interconnected whole of reality as one living, breathing, organism. This, Rabbi Natan teaches, is the very essence of *shalom*, of peace, for it is at that moment that we are able to realize the *sheleimut* of all life.

6   **peace in true perfection.** Here I have translated the word *sheleimut* as "perfection," though it could certainly also carry the valence of "wholeness" indicated in the previous chapter.

It is the aspect of
"There is none like you, our Savior,
at the resurrection of the dead"
[ve-'ein domeh leikha moshi'einu lithiyat ha-meitim]
that we recite on Shabbat.[4]
For the Sabbath is a semblance of the world to come—
the aspect of the resurrection of the dead—
for [in that time] people will live an eternal life
in body and in soul ...

There is always discord [mahloket] between the soul and the body,
and from there flows all the different kinds of discord
that exist in the world.
Thus there can be no peace except when [people] merit to have
their souls overpower their bodies.[5]
The body will be inverted into soul [she-yit-hapeikh ha-guf le-nefesh],
and that is peace in true perfection
[she-'az hu' ha-shalom bi-sheleimut be-'emet].[6]

(continued on page 143)

7 **as it is written.** Isaiah 11:6.

The righteous merit to break the body entirely [*leshabeir ha-guf le-gamrei*],
to the point that the physical will is nullified completely
and it actually inverts into a soul.
For this is the essence of peace [*'ikar ha-shalom*],
as we mentioned above.
And so too in the future to come,
when everyone will merit this—
then there will be a wondrous peace in the world,
as it is written: "The wolf will dwell with the lamb ..."[7]

As Though All My Work Is Done

Master of the world,
let me merit the joy and freedom
of the holy Shabbat,
and let me nullify the
enslavement of the days of the week.

I pray that my mind will be completely settled,
without any confusion at all—
and that on the holy Sabbath
no thoughts of labor and business,
nor any worry or trouble,
will enter my mind.

Rather it will be in my eyes
as though all my work is done.
Then I will have truly attained
the rest and pleasure and joy
of the holy Sabbath.

Likutei Tefilot 2:13

Awareness of God

1 **the inwardness of divine vitality.** Here the homilist makes use of a classic Hebrew wordplay to convey a profound spiritual insight. The world as we perceive it is a veil, a state of concealment within which the deeper truth of divine reality is contained. The common Hebrew root of *ayin-lamed-mem* is interpreted to indicate that the character of the world is an essential hiddenness; it is called *'olam* precisely because it constitutes a state of *he-'elem*, of concealment in which the divine core of reality is wrapped in its outer garb. At some frequency in his commentary, R. Yehudah Leib asserts a dichotomy between the world of nature (*ha-teva'*) and the realm beyond nature (*le-ma'alah min ha-teva'*)—the physical domain as we experience it and the eternal spirit of Divinity that dwells within. In many instances, Shabbat itself is referred to as being *le-ma'alah min ha-teva'*—the Sabbath constitutes the timeless transcendence within the rhythms of ordinary time. This is also a statement about the *Sefat 'Emet*'s view of divine immanence—the idea that God is to be found *within* the world, not beyond it (transcendence). The *penimiyut* (inwardness) of Divinity is a living force that resides in the deepest center of all reality, in the core of the human heart, in the vessel of nature.

Sefer Sefat 'Emet

Rabbi Yehudah Leib Alter of Ger

Truly the world [*ha-'olam*]
was named for the hiddenness [*ha-he'elem*],
insofar as the natural realm [*ha-teva'*]
conceals the inwardness of divine vitality
[*mekhaseh penimiyut ḥiyut 'Elohut*].[1]

(*continued on page 151*)

149

2 **the contraction of nature.** Despite the fact that God is always present as the great life-force within, the outer veils of the world make it impossible for human beings to perceive that Presence. We live inevitably in a state of obstruction in which the deep truth of existence is imperceptible to us. Only when the veil of nature is contracted, only when that cover is drawn back, can we reach awareness of the divine truth within. The physical domain of nature is thus both a vessel for the divine inwardness and an obstacle to ultimate mystical awareness. But isn't this a counterintuitive claim for those of us who find spiritual majesty in the *teva'* itself, in the stuff of nature? Don't we stand before the wonders of the natural with the radical amazement that Abraham Joshua Heschel spoke of so passionately? Surely we can say with the naturalist John Muir that the wilderness is a divine temple! The teaching offered by the Gerer Rebbe, however, implies that we must train ourselves to see the world through the eyes of spiritual sight. When properly cultivated, the consciousness of the mystic beholds the world not just as a thing of great beauty, but as an embodiment of the sacred. For at the same time that the physical world is a veil of concealment for the divine *penimiyut*, it is also the primary pathway into that inwardness; the garment that hides is simultaneously the door that reveals. It all depends on the awareness with which we approach it.

3 **the heavens and the earth.** If the days of the workweek, Sunday through Friday, are the time of concealment and obstructed awareness, Shabbat is the time of opened consciousness, the moment when the Jew achieves a new state of *hakarah* (recognition/awareness) of the Divine. This new spiritual perception is framed by the *Sefat 'Emet* as "the ultimate purpose of creation"—the underlying aim of the world's being is the ability of the Jew to know the Creator, the possibility that we may come to realize the deep truth of existence. For this reason was Shabbat called the "culmination and final purpose of Creation" (a formulation that was canonized in poetic form in the Friday evening liturgy)—for Shabbat is the time when the mind is opened in a way like no other. All of life, all of reality, is oriented toward this great end—that we may come closer to God, that the doors of perception may be opened to realize that the *penimiyut* of Divinity fills all.

And truly all of creation
is just for His glory, may His name be blessed.
But it is impossible to recognize the Creator
['iy 'efshar lehakir 'et ha-borei],
may His name be blessed,
except through the contraction of nature
[rak 'al yedei tzimtzum ha-teva'].[2]
Through His actions [people] can recognize Him;
through the physical concealment,
recognition of His Divinity comes to be.

And Shabbat is the recognition of Divinity [hakarat ha-'Elohut],
which is the ultimate purpose of creation
[she-hi takhlit ha-beriah],
and it is called the purpose/completion
of the heavens and the earth [takhlit shamayim va-'aretz].[3]

(continued on page 153)

4   **came to rest on him.** Isaiah 11:2. In a wonderful play on words, the *menuḥah* (rest) of Shabbat is equated with a state of prophetic consciousness. This play turns on the sense of a prophetic spirit coming to rest upon the person (*ve-naḥah 'alav ruaḥ YHVH*). In this sense, *menuḥah* is not simply a cessation of activity; it is also a state of inspiration, an influx of the divine spirit. A heightened state of perception is attained on Shabbat, one that is tied directly to the indwelling of an otherworldly force of prophecy in the person. As presented here, the act of *menuḥah* is not the physical rest we normally associate with the Sabbath—instead, it is a state of being "rested upon" by the divine spirit, receiving the emanating energies from Above such that one's mind becomes a vessel filled with the consciousness-expanding force of God. We are able to reach a transcendent plane of awareness on Shabbat—a state of mind in which the ground of Being opens to us as heavenly revelation, in which we suddenly become able to dwell within the eternal and the infinite, to ascend beyond the arc of human time.

5   **to refer to prophecy.** *Mekhilta, Parashat Bo, Hakdamah.*

6   **will be prophets.** In this culminating moment of the commentary, the *Sefat 'Emet* associates the transformed awareness of Shabbat— the inspired prophetic state in which the truth of Divinity is perceived—with the kabbalistic notion of the extra soul (*neshamah yeteirah*) that dwells in the Jew during the holy Sabbath. The force of Divinity that comes to rest upon us (*ve-naḥah 'alav ruaḥ YHVH*), infusing us with an opened consciousness, is none other than the extra soul itself.

This is the aspect of rest [*behinat menuhah*],
which [in turn] is the aspect of prophecy
and the holy spirit [*behinat nevu'ah ve-ruah ha-kodesh*].
As it is written:
"The spirit of *YHVH* came to rest on him
[*ve-nahah 'alav ruah YHVH*]."[4]

And so too did our Sages interpret [the words]
"and I have not found rest [*u-menuhah lo matzati*]"
to refer to prophecy [*nevu'ah*].[5]
This is the aspect of the extra soul
[*zeh behinat neshamah yeteirah*],
a semblance of the world to come,
when all of the people of God will be prophets....[6]

(*continued on page 155*)

7 **it is called *ḥilul Shabbat*.** As we have seen in earlier texts, this use of the phrase *ḥilul Shabbat*, a standard expression to characterize the violation of the Sabbath laws, here seems to carry a double meaning. On Shabbat, the holy divine energies dwell in the world, but through the introduction of weekday actions (*melakhah*/labor), that divine presence departs, leaving behind an absence—a space devoid of the holy spirit. As such the hasidic master puns upon the word *ḥilul*, evoking thereby an alliterative correlation to the word *ḥalal* (space)—a word most prominently used in Lurianic Kabbalah in the context of the *ḥalal panui*, the empty space that is left in primordial reality after the Infinite withdraws to make space for the finite world to exist. Thus, the performance of labor on Shabbat causes the holy spirit to withdraw, leaving the world empty and parched.

Therefore labor on Shabbat
was prohibited for the children of Israel,
since the ultimate purpose of labor and weekday action is
to serve as a vessel so that the energies of holiness
may dwell upon creation;
all the days of the workweek are preparation for Shabbat,
and through labor [melakhah] on the seventh day
the holy spirit departs, and it is called ḥilul Shabbat
["desecration of the Sabbath"].[7]

Thus it was through Shabbat and menuḥah
that the work of Creation was completed.
For this [the arrival of Shabbat and menuḥah]
is the ultimate purpose of melakhah, as mentioned above.

Song and Peace

May we merit to sing and make melody before You—
melodies, songs, and praises for the sake of Your name,
and to worship You always in truth—

until we merit, through Your compassion,
to arouse the Song of Songs that King Solomon composed—
a song greater than all other songs—
and until we merit to attain all ten forms of melody
about which the book of Psalms spoke.

Bless us with Your benevolent peace,
and send the flow of peace onto Your people Israel forever—
that there be peace among all of Israel,
between a person and his friend,
between husband and wife.

Let this peace grow
until it is drawn upon all dwellers of the world.

And let us merit to receive
a Sabbath of peace with great joy,
and spread over us the shelter of Your peace.

Likutei Tefilot 1:27

Uniting the Physical and the Spiritual

1 **the work that He had done.** Genesis 2:2.

2 **he states.** This is a statement drawn directly from the rabbinic midrash *Bereishit Rabbah* 10:9. It was a common practice of this legendary medieval interpreter to transmit traditions from the Late Antique midrashim.

3 **the work of Creation.** Already in the midrashic text the language of the biblical verse was troubling. Why does the narrator in Genesis state that the Creation was completed on the seventh day (Shabbat) if that was the day of rest (*va-yekhal 'Elohim ba-yom ha-shevi'i*)? Wasn't the last creation enacted on the sixth day? The ancient Rabbis resolved this interpretive difficulty by asserting that rest itself was the final creation; the essence of the Sabbath was the necessary completion of the previous six days of Creation. *Menuḥah* is thus understood to be an essential and fundamental component of the created reality; the Sabbath contributes something crucial to the balance of existence.

4 **the holy Sabbath.** Here the hasidic rabbi explains that the reason for the creation of the human being on the sixth day, when it was actually deemed fitting to create the person on the Sabbath itself, is that the human being is a unique combination of the physical and the spiritual. The human condition is one of living in between—of dwelling in the mundane realm of bodies and desires at the same time that we cultivate a life of the spirit and the soul. And this is represented by the tension between the six days of the week and the holy Sabbath. The days of ordinary time (*ḥol*) correspond to the domain of physicality, while the Sabbath is the day of the soul, the time of pure spirit and holiness (*kodesh*). In our situation on the border between these two time frames, we are able to serve as a bridge between two opposing orders of being, to create an integrated fusion between them. In the person, the sacred and the ordinary are welded together; as finite creatures who dwell within mortal bodies, we are ever bound to our experience of the physical, the world of *ḥol*. And yet, within those bodily garments, we are also illumined by an eternal soul, a spark of Divinity whose light flows from the Endless. The human

(*continued on page 162*)

Sefer Sefat 'Emet

Rabbi Yehudah Leib Alter of Ger

In Rashi's commentary on the verse
"And on the seventh day God completed the work
that He had done
[va-yekhal 'Elohim ba-yom ba-shevi'i
melakhto 'asher 'asah],"[1]
he states:[2]
Shabbat arrived, and rest arrived,
completing the work of Creation.[3]

For it mentions a creative act [melakhah]
that was supposed to have been performed on Shabbat.
But instead the actions on the sixth day were doubled,
and the action intended for the seventh day
was performed on the sixth.
For on the sixth day two creations were made:
animals and the human being.

It would have been fitting
for the creation of the human being
to have taken place on the holy Shabbat.
And the explanation is that the human being
contains both physicality and spirituality
[de-'adam yesh bo gashmiyut ve-ruhaniyut],
and he is a binding together of
the days of the week with the holy Sabbath.[4]

(continued on page 163)

being could have been created on the Sabbath itself, the rabbi avers, precisely because we contain *ruḥaniyut* (spirituality/spiritual substance). This spiritual essence, reflected in the soul, is what makes the person possess a kinship with the very nature of the Sabbath—the spiritual substance of the Sabbath is of a piece with the soul of the person. For this reason, the mystics claim, the Sabbath is a unique time in which an extra soul (*neshamah yeteirah*) descends from heaven to dwell within the Jew. And so, the human being is the one creature capable of bridging the physicality of workaday time with the pure spirituality of Sabbath time—to bring the entirety of existence, body and soul, into harmony and reunion.

5　**why the Sages asked.** Jerusalem Talmud, *Sanhedrin* 23b.

6　**to the upper world.** The spiritual seeker unites heaven and earth with a yearning for the heart of Being; in entering into the Sabbath, we are able to lift the world of the body into the transcendent space of the holy. But it is also through the created world, through the physical, that we are able to reach toward the sacred, to "cleave to the upper world." Despite the polarity between the sacred and the ordinary, spirit and body, they are organically bound one to the other. The very fact of our situation in the physical realm is necessary to our path into the spiritual. And in this we may discover a profound lesson. We need not—indeed, we *must* not—build a barrier between our physical lives and our spiritual lives. Ours is a condition of integration, in which the paths of the mundane, of all we may learn in the life of ordinary things, may lead to the recognition of deep spiritual truths. Through the world of nature and earthiness, through our connection to the wonders of the body and the mysteries of mortality, of all that grows from and returns to the earth—through these things we may arrive at moments of true revelation. Through this world we may come to a new condition of Sabbath consciousness— one that is the ultimate destiny of our humanity, a fulfillment of our createdness on the sixth day, on the edge of the Sabbath.

7　**the work of Creation that He had done.** Genesis 2:2.

This is why the Sages asked:[5]
Why was the human being created last?
So that he could enter immediately into Shabbat.
The meaning of this is:
The human being binds together all of creation,
and through all of them [the creations]
he cleaves to the upper world.[6]

This is what was written:
"He rested from all the work of Creation
that He had done
[shavat mi-kol melakhto 'asher bara' 'Elohim la'asot].[7]

(continued on page 165)

8 **made it holy.** Genesis 2:3. The arrival of Shabbat on the seventh day of Creation was not merely a cessation of divine activity, a resting from the labor of the first six days. Instead, the Sabbath is understood to be the essence of all created reality; it is the divine force that gives life and sustenance to the physical world. The bestowal of holiness, which was first given by God in the act of Creation, is the influx of divine spirit into the earthly realm, the indwelling of the soul to the body of physical reality. In the words of the rabbi, the Sabbath is "the essence of the existence of the world," the spiritual lifeblood that courses through the veins of mundane being. Sabbath rest is not a passive state; it is the fountain of all that lives and breathes—the waters of holiness that flow from the depths of Divinity and nourish the parched soil of our physical reality.

How are we to understand this imprinting of the Sabbath "form" onto the landscape of matter? How may we recover this image in our day? It is the Sabbath—filled with the tones and reverberations of ancient time, the echoes of the divine voice at Sinai commanding us to "remember" and to "keep," the sounds of family and the intoxicating smell of baking *hallah* on Friday afternoons, the twilight air and the earthen streets of shtetls long swept away into the passage of generations and destruction. It is the Sabbath—the enchanted pathways of golden light, the space within time in which we *remember*. A remembering of all that is still good and hopeful in our world, a remembering of the melody and the peace that brings us back to our spiritual center amidst a life so often oppressed by the rush of deadlines and the burdens of the body. In this magical time, this glimpse of the world to come, we keep the memory of that which is truly meaningful in our lives, allowing it to spread over us as a shelter of peace—*ha-pores sukkat shalom 'aleinu ve-'al kol Yisra'el.*

The spiritual force of the Sabbath, the holiness that it contains, gives shape and meaning to the physical terrain of this world. It is "the form that is imprinted upon the matter," the seal that distinguishes the ring of the king. In the earthly reality, the dominion of God, the Sabbath is the true marker of the divine presence, the ultimate signifier of the creative force of Divinity. The spiritual power of the Sabbath lifts matter out of an undifferentiated stream, inscribes it with the imprint of ultimate meaning, the signature of God.

This is to say that the creation of physicality [*gashmiyut*]
ceased on the Sabbath,
but the essence of the existence of the world
is the Sabbath, and this is the holiness—
"and He made it holy
[*va-yekadesh 'oto*]"⁸—
with that which is spirituality,
the form that is imprinted upon the matter.

(*continued on page 167*)

9 **in the midrash.** *Bereishit Rabbah* 10:9.

10 **the Creator, blessed be He.** As we saw in an earlier text from the *Sefat 'Emet*, the Sabbath is a time of transformed spiritual awareness, a recognition of the divine presence in a way unlike all other times.

This was hinted at by the Sages in the midrash,[9]
in the parable of the ring that was missing a seal.
Shabbat arrived, and the seal was made—
for all of God's actions
were for the sake of the Sabbath.

It follows that this recognition [*hakarah zot*],
in which the creatures recognize
that He created it all for His glory,
and they nullify themselves to Him, may He be blessed—
this is the establishment, the support
of the world [*zeh kiyum ha-'olam*],
and this is accomplished on Shabbat,
when the children of Israel
give witness to the Creator, blessed be He.[10]

◆ For the most part I have sought to avoid commenting on these selections from Reb Natan's *Likutei Tefilot,* in an effort to let them stand on their own as focused devotional moments. I have wanted to encourage you, the reader, to make spiritual use of these brief, spontaneous prayers without the filter of my commentary, and I have selected lines to translate that can be appreciated without much mediation. This prayer, however, cries out for more interpretation "between the lines." Here Rabbi Natan offers a reflection that might be correlated to his remarks in the prayer I titled "Song and Peace" above: singing is understood to constitute a powerful and elevating mode of spiritual practice, one that can awaken the individual's devotional bond to Divinity, lifting the person up to a state of transformed spiritual awareness. This is, of course, a devotional rendering of Rabbi Naḥman of Bratzlav's teachings in his *Likutei Moharan. Nigun*—melody—is a spiritual technique for drawing closer to God and opening the mind to new mystical perception.

Here Rabbi Natan continues this thread of Rabbi Naḥman's thought, emphasizing that we yearn to attain a state of pure joy on Shabbat and in our ongoing worship of the Holy One. And we seek to bind ourselves to the elevating power of the *nigun* that may carry us to that place of pure *simḥah,* pure happiness.[1]

Sorrow and lament are frequently viewed by Rabbi Naḥman and his disciples as the enemies of higher spiritual attainment—itself a perspective that is deeply revealing of the rabbi's internal emotional struggles with depression and sadness.[2]

It is unclear exactly who Rabbi Natan had in mind with the statement "melodies of wailing and sadness that the wicked ones sing most of the time," but such sorrowful singing was clearly considered to have a harmful effect upon the quest to draw closer to Divinity. These *nigunim* of lament capture the hearts of ordinary people, Rabbi Natan asserts—a remark that is almost as fascinating as the fear of sorrowful melodies itself. Why are the ordinary folk so drawn to such song? Does it resonate with their existential angst? Their sense of the tragic in everyday life?

But the disciple of Rabbi Naḥman does not stop there. He does not merely exhort his readers to shut out this sorrowful song, to suppress the appeal it presents. Instead, he offers a solution that is much more akin to the approach that the earliest hasidic masters took to dealing

The Power of Melody

Master of the world,
Guardian of Your people Israel forever—
guard and save us that we not be drawn after
melodies of wailing and sadness
that the wicked ones sing most of the time,
and to which ordinary people are most drawn.

Help us always to bring joy to our souls
in holiness and purity
through melodies and songs of joy
that draw the heart to You—
to Your worship, to Your Torah,
and to Your righteous ones in truth.

Help us through the power of the true *tzaddikim*,
that we may merit to elevate
all those melodies of the wicked
through the holiness of Shabbat—
that You might give us the strength to elevate them
and to invert them into joy
when we sing them on the holy Sabbath.

(continued on page 171)

with distracting, inappropriate thoughts during prayer: raise them up to their source of holiness and purity! Descend into the depths of dangerous temptation in order to lift up the fallen in a drama of redemption, to ascend even higher to the realm of divine perfection. In this prayer, Rabbi Natan states that the power of Shabbat offers a remarkable opportunity: through the Sabbath's unique force, we may enter into these sorrowful melodies and transform them into channels of joy and happiness! As he articulates it, "Help us through the power of the true *tzaddikim*, that we may merit to elevate all those melodies of the wicked through the holiness of Shabbat—that You might give us the strength to elevate them and to invert them into joy *when we sing them on the holy Sabbath.*" We *should* sing these songs of lament, these melodies that evoke sorrow—but because of the power of Shabbat we will be able to transform and invert them.

What, however, do we think of this advice in our own time and place? So much of our experience of prayer is saturated with the rhythms of music. And surely music holds the power to evoke particular emotional moods—both as representation (what the music communicates) and as inspiration (what emotions the music evokes in us, affecting our state of spiritual experience). But must we always aspire to an ideal of joy in the act of devotion? And do we say with Rabbi Natan that the sorrow-laden melodies should be transformed into joyous song on the Sabbath?

It would seem that even the Bratzlav master and disciple recognized the power of the melody that evokes a mood of lament, despite the fact that they sought to resist it. Major and minor keys stimulate distinctly different emotions and spiritual states within us, and if the melodies in major have the force to lift us up to a celebratory ecstasy, a swoon of the spirit, the *nigunim* in minor take us to a more contemplative space, a brooding alignment with the mystery of existence. The melody in minor may be sorrow-haunted and still be more effective in accessing that meditative region of the spirit—the mood of such music is indeed a deep cry of the soul, a yearning for the secret of Creation dwelling as darkness over the face of an inner deep. The contemplative melody lifts us to the plane where souls meet and merge, where we sense the looming oneness of our breath and the spirit of the world.

The merit of Shabbat will protect us,
such that those melodies will not have the power
to draw forth sadness, heaven forbid.

On the contrary,
we will only merit to purify and elevate them—
to invert them from sorrow and lament
into joy and celebration!

Likutei Tefilot 1:138

Concluding Meditations

Each of the six days anticipates the Shabbat to which it leads. Just as the days of the week prior to Shabbat are considered to be a part of that coming Sabbath's Torah portion (and the first lines of that Sabbath's Torah reading are read in the synagogue on the Monday and Thursday of the week before), so too are those six days understood to be bound up in that coming Sabbath's spiritual substance. Each of those weekdays receives its flow of holiness, its essential energy, from the Shabbat that it anticipates. Collectively, they are the body, and Shabbat is their soul. Thus are we commanded to "remember the Sabbath day in order to sanctify it" (*zakhor et yom ha-shabbat le-kaddsho*). That act of remembering is a daily spiritual practice in which we bring to mind the way in which this particular day (the one in which we find ourselves) is rooted in the coming Shabbat. It is *yom ri'shon be-shabbat*—the first day (i.e., Sunday)— that is *of the coming Sabbath*. It is anchored in the Sabbath that is anticipated. It is part and parcel of that Sabbath's spiritual energy, and every thought and action of that day must be aligned with the Shabbat that stands at its source.

How is our attitude different during the six days of the week as we contemplate their rootedness in the anticipated Shabbat? How might the promise of Shabbat offer us an anchor of intention for our behaviors and our thoughts from Sunday to Friday? As we learned from R. Tzadok ha-Kohen, the weekdays are sustained and nourished by their connection to the Sabbath source; we must move through the practice of our everyday lives with an ongoing awareness of the fountain of blessing that flows into those ordinary moments. In living with such a heightened awareness, with such a focused state of mindfulness, we truly effect the sanctification of the ordinary. Each day becomes a fulfillment of the command to sanctify the Sabbath day through an act of remembrance, an act of *zakhor*.

Remembering the Sabbath may be understood as a kind of mental intention, a focusing of the mind on the deeper meaning of time as we experience it in the ebb and flow of the work week. Our goal is to achieve a state of Sabbath awareness, where we recall how the life we live in ordinary time is an organic outflow of the life of holy time. Each moment can be traced back to its source in the life-giving energy of the Sabbath, in the soul of weekday time.

☙❧

The hasidic masters teach that each week constitutes a special and incomparable unit in the fabric of Being and time. A unique creation, the individual week stands on its own as something of deep significance—it is not simply absorbed into the sweeping flow of the calendar, week in and week out. Shabbat is not rest and cessation; it is the energy source for the contained organism of the seven-day unit. For just as it is a *zeikher le-ma'aseh bereishit*—a remembrance of the act of Creation—so too it is the force of renewal that animates our lives, a fresh beginning that opens into new possibilities and new responsibilities. Each week is a treasure unto itself, a dimension of reality and experience that has never before been in this world. We must therefore approach life as it unfolds in each new week as filled with wonder and illumination, mystery, and anticipation. To be aware of the true renewal of Shabbat and its six days is to be open to the untraveled road that beckons at the gateway of this new creation. By receiving each Sabbath as a renewal, we come to realize the preciousness and fragility of every moment, the power of a new beginning to raise our awareness of the sacred, and of all that needs repair and transformation in our lives. Attaining this mindfulness may lead us to a new embrace of repentance and self-examination, an approach of true compassion toward the others we encounter on the path of time.

❧

The renewal of the created world extends to include a renewal within the person, all of which is made possible through the redemptive power of Shabbat. Even if those six days are a time of darkness and great challenge, the hasidic mystics assert, remember that the Sabbath holds the power to raise you out of your state of misery, to bring healing and redemption to even the most desperate and despairing. A semblance of the world to come, Shabbat is a glimpse of perfection. And in opening ourselves to that otherworldly force—in receiving the Sabbath as the groom receives the bride—we allow the power of redemption to enter into our deepest selves, to infuse our despair with the life-giving energy of a new soul from the divine realm. Shabbat is a fountain of hope, the promise that we can be raised from even the lowliest of places, the dream that we can heal and rebuild from even the most profound state of brokenness.

And how does Shabbat have that power? What is it about the seventh day that can promise such redemption? For the spiritual masters, the Sabbath as we know it is an indwelling of the divine presence from Above. Divinity becomes manifest through this wondrous moment in time, and so infuses the world with the blessing of spiritual mystery, with the flowing river of eternal light. We must learn to become present to that force of rest and restoration, to receive it into our hearts and our souls, a *kabbalat Shabbat* true and deep. Whatever the pain and suffering that we carry all week long, Shabbat offers us the chance to release that pressure for a time, to transcend our limiting enslavement to pettiness and greed, to pride and strife. On Shabbat, in the company of love and friendship, we may experience the redemption of hope, the liberation of peace.

The Sabbath is the stabilizing force of all that is. And just as Creation was incomplete without the introduction of rest into the world, so too reality needs the peace of Shabbat in order to exist. The Sabbath peace is a cosmic energy bestowed by God. It is the equilibrium and harmonizing element of all Being.

◈

Shabbat shalom! What is the meaning of this "peace" that we associate with the Sabbath? As the hasidic mystics teach, we should not think of peace as merely the absence of violence, discord, and conflict. It is that, to be sure, but it is first and foremost a positive force in and of itself. *Shalom* is a flux of energy, a pulse of divine being that courses through the rivulets of life and time. Peace is a blessing that is bestowed, an overflow of divine emanation that blankets all reality with tranquility and centeredness. When we receive the gift of *shalom*, we are reconnected to our deepest anchor, to the orienting ground of our existence. And this peace—this sheltering—is the cosmic force of Shabbat. For just as there is Shabbat in this world, so too is there the dimension of Shabbat within the divine Self. It is the ultimate register of calm and perfection. Its entrance into our time on the seventh day offers us a glimpse of what is possible in a world redeemed.

The challenge of the spiritual quest is to release the turmoil of *maḥloket* (discord, contention) within ourselves, and to open ourselves up to receive the gift of peace from above. The peace we speak of is not just the resolution of interpersonal and international conflict. It is those things too, but the guiding state of *shalom* must begin in the inner regions of our own selves, in our hearts and in our minds. We must learn to let go of the competitions and the bitterness that eat away at our emotional and physical health. We must allow ourselves release from the tight grip of egoism and pride, from grudges and anger, from obsessions with pettiness and selfishness that keep us locked in the prison of an inner violence, resentment, and anger. The peace that comes to dwell within us on Shabbat is a vision of the equilibrium that we seek throughout the six days of ordinary time.

The calming energy of Sabbath peace fills the world at sundown on Friday, and it is this tranquility that we hope to retain through one last inhalation of the spices during *Havdalah* on Saturday night. But even the Sabbath cannot fill our hearts with peace if we keep them stubbornly guarded and obstructed! This is the true meaning of *kabbalat Shabbat*, the reception of the Sabbath on Friday evening. We must open our hearts to the flow that streams from the Source of all blessing and all holiness. We must face the luminous presence of Shabbat with souls turned open to the serenity of the hour. *Likrat Shabbat lekhu ve-neilekhah, ki hi mekor ha-berakhah,* "Toward the Sabbath let us go forth, for she is the source of blessing!" *Penei Shabbat nekabbelah,* "Let us receive the face of the Sabbath!"

Shabbat is the time when the barriers of perception fall away, when the *shalom* of Shabbat bestows a vision of *sheleimut,* the oneness and whole-ness of all Being. *Shema!* Hear, O Israel, our God is the sublime Oneness of all that is! This is the ultimate moment of prayer, the experience upon which all devotion is based: to be at one with the organic force of all life, to be opened to the presence of God so completely that all divisions disappear, and it is only the blessed name forever and ever (*barukh shem kevod malkhuto le-olam va-'ed*). This climactic moment is expressed in the subsequent paragraph of the *Shema* as well: to love God with all your heart, all your soul, and all your strength is to break open the walls that enclose your fragile heart and soul, keeping it far from the brilliance of the world outside. To be fully present to God is to pour out your heart, to free it of all the pent-up resentments and regrets that fester inside like incubating toxins. Then the *Shema* is the long exhalation of deep medi-tative release. We send the breath out, emptying our minds and our souls of all that keeps us from the restorative light of the sacred. In the *Shema,* our breath becomes one with the Source.

The human being is a microcosm for the very nature of Being. Our bodies are composed of many different parts and elements, but all are interdependent pieces of a single organism. For even though we may speak of limbs or organs as individual entities, can they really be defined apart from the whole? The soul is the divine force that animates this physical self, uniting it as a living being. So, too, in the created universe. Though it may appear that this world is composed of separate, inde-pendent elements, the deeper truth is that it is all one and inseparable from the life-force of Divinity. We need only wake ourselves up to this fundamental realization, this theological awareness that the seeming manifold character of the world is but a mask for the secret of oneness. The *Shema* is the devotional call to this awakening. It is the cry at the heart of the spiritual life that opens our eyes to the truth that God *is* Being; Divinity is the All, and we are but the outer marks of particularity inscribed in the complete circle of divine unity.

The splendor of Shabbat awakens our yearning for God—we are as lovers entering the wedding canopy. It is the sacred time of the Sabbath that stirs us to fulfill the command of the *Shema*, "you shall love God with all your heart," and we are moved to a deeper level of devotion than we are able to reach within the bounds of the ordinary. There is an intangible quality to our encounter with the sacred—senses opened to the sublime, the heart called to purpose and direction. In the restorative airs of Shabbat, our hearts are opened to the flow of divine love, the world is filled with possibility: in the echoes of an ancient song of courtship and desire, we receive the spirit and send it forth. The mystics of old would go out to the fields to receive the Sabbath bride in the twilight of working time. She is the force of rest and blessing that gives breath to nature; she is the face of Shabbat, the light of the Other World.

Community and fellowship have the power to lift us beyond our ordinary natures, indeed beyond the very confines of the natural order. The phrase *'al tiv'i*, beyond nature, is one that we also see with some frequency in the writings of the Gerer rebbe, the *Sefat 'Emet*. There Shabbat is characterized as a dimension of reality that reaches beyond the edges of ordinary time and space. Shabbat is *le-ma'alah mei-ha-zeman u-le-ma'alah mei-ha-teva'*, beyond time and beyond nature. It evokes something of the otherworldly, a plane of spiritual reality that touches the rim of heaven, transcending the regular structures and forms by which we know and measure existence.

And yet, many hasidic mystics invoked the famous *gematria* (alphanumerical meaning and correlation), already known to Spinoza, in which one of the dominant divine names (*'Elohim*/אלֹהים) is equated with the Hebrew word for nature (*ha-teva*/הטבע). Through this interpretive move, various mystical thinkers sought to underscore the belief that God is to be found within the natural world. Or dare we say that nature is part of the divine essence?

We might expect the mystic to say that one requires seclusion and meditative retreat from other people in order to attain the heights of spiritual experience and encounter with Divinity. But several hasidic teachers assert that individuality and solitude will get one only so far. To reach for the summit of the spiritual quest, a person must become bonded to the life and energy of a community. That *koah ha-rabim* (the power of the multitude, the strength of community) holds the force of mystical transcendence, where a person can break through the boundaries of ordinary physicality and natural law. The limitations of our natures are conquered through the collective elevation of devotional fellowship, and this is the rarefied condition that we seek on Shabbat. Individual contemplation and devotional practice are of great value, but it is through the energy of togetherness that we are able to climb to new rungs on the ladder.

What is it about community that allows us to reach beyond ourselves in a way that we cannot in solitude? Carried on the tide of melody—now contemplative, then ecstatic—we are transported to another spiritual region of consciousness and feeling. The thunderclap of Sinai pounds within us once again, reverberating in the interconnected caves of time. In the hands of spiritual fellowship, our souls become buoyant and new, able to reach beyond the shapes created by language and tradition. It is through that force of community that we are lifted to a new plane of spiritual consciousness and feeling. The boundaries of physical existence are effaced, and we are able to touch the mystery of the Great Beyond.

Slowly, almost imperceptibly, the late afternoon light begins to unravel—the hour of separation is approaching. Soon the mystery of the seventh day will yield again to the pressures of this world, the realm of souls giving way to ordinary time. For as much as it holds the eternal, Shabbat is also elusive, ever returning us to the mundane rhythms of life. And this is necessary: for it then awakens in us the yearning for that center of calm, that restoration of stillness in our innermost selves.

The dusk throws its otherworldly shadows over the land and the city. We can feel the retreat of the Sabbath Queen, her return to the place of light above. The flame of the *Havdalah* candle burns bright with its converging strands, offering us a glimpse of the world redeemed. And the spices we inhale are sustenance to the soul as it releases the Sabbath energy; we draw that scent inward, a marker of the *ruah*, the spirit, that dwells in the seventh day.

A new week begins, unfolding to undiscovered land, the Sabbath both memory and dream. In entering and exiting the sacred time, we are travelers into the terrain of the eternal and the timeless. For the spark of this day shines with the light of a world beyond our experience, and still with the vitality of generations gone by. Years, centuries, millennia: the candles lit, the food prepared, the prayers said. We can almost hear the voices of unknown ancestors, resounding over the deep well of time.

The Sabbath is ever-renewed, mysterious, and surprising, even as it arrives like a familiar old friend. *Likrat Shabbat lekhu ve-neilkhah*: Let us go forth again to greet the Sabbath in the fields and on the pathways of this earth. She is the always present soul of our ordinary lives, calling to us from beneath the veils of existence, leading us on our quest for spiritual purpose in this world.

Acknowledgments

A s I send this book off into the world, I am grateful to the many individuals who contributed to my thinking on this subject. Most formatively, I want to thank my many students at The Jewish Theological Seminary (JTS) who studied a number of these texts with me in seminars devoted to the Sabbath in hasidic thought, and whose questions and insights nuanced and deepened my own approach to the material. My appreciation to all of you.

Several of these thoughts were also first presented to a wonderful group of colleagues who gathered together three times at Princeton University for the Working Group on Holiness, hosted and sponsored by the Tikvah Project on Jewish Thought at Princeton. Special thanks to Prof. Alan Mittleman, valued colleague and mentor at JTS, who convened and chaired the group, as well as to Prof. Leora Batnitzky, director of the Tikvah Project at Princeton, her excellent assistant, Gabriella Wertman, and the Tikvah Fund for its support of that stimulating intellectual experience. I am also grateful to the other members of that working group: Prof. Eliezer Diamond, Prof. Jon Jacobs, Prof. Elsie Stern, Prof. Isaac Lifshitz, Prof. Sharon Portnoy, and Nina Redl, for a very rich conversation and for sharpening my reflections through collegial dialogue.

For their support and feedback on this project, I am grateful to: Rabbi Bradley Shavit Artson, Rabbi David Ellenson, Rabbi Laura Geller, Prof. Arthur Green, Jay Greenspan, Prof. Susannah Heschel, Rabbi Lawrence Kushner, Prof. Vivian Mann, Rabbi Daniel Nevins, Rabbi Marcia Prager, Prof. Raymond Scheindlin, Ms. Irene Zwerling Schenck, Rabbi Jonathan Slater, Rabbi Sheila Peltz Weinberg, Dr. Ron Wolfson, and Rabbi David Wolpe.

Sincere thanks to Sharon Lieberman-Mintz, curator of Jewish Art at the Library of The Jewish Theological Seminary, for her expert and generous help in locating treasures within that extraordinary collection. Thanks as well to Prof. David Kraemer, librarian of the Seminary, and Rabbi Jerry Schwarzbard, librarian for special collections at JTS, for granting me permission to publish an image from a manuscript held in the Seminary's rare collections. For swift and courteous administrative help with the library materials, I am grateful to: Sarah Diamant, Yevgeniya Dizenko, and Hector Guzman.

Once again the terrific folks at Jewish Lights Publishing have been a delight to work with. I am grateful for their insight and professionalism at every stage of the publication process, and for their openness to my preferences and ideas throughout. Special thanks to Stuart Matlins, publisher and founder of Jewish Lights; Emily Wichland, vice president of Editorial and Production; Lauren Hill, project editor; and Jennifer Rataj, publicist; as well as to Debra Corman for her keen eye at copy editing.

On a more personal note, it is a great pleasure to recognize my daughter, Aderet Fishbane. Aderet is a constant source of wonder and blessing in my life. She sparkles with the light of *Shabbes*; the *neshamah yeteirah* shines brightly in her sweet and loving face.

I am also deeply grateful to my wife, Rabbi Julia Andelman, for all that she does to fill our home with warmth and love. It is a great joy to share the peace of Shabbat with such an *eshet ḥayil*, each week a sanctuary and a blessing.

My earliest childhood memories center on the Shabbat table of my parents, Dr. Mona DeKoven Fishbane and Prof. Michael Fishbane—a space of blessing that I shared with my brother, Elisha. I can still see my mother preparing for Shabbat and lighting the candles; I can see my father holding the Kiddush cup, chanting the words with the melody that I have now passed on to my daughter. Passionate conversations with the many guests who joined us for the Friday night meal; the pleasure of walking to shul together; of studying Torah and singing as the shadows grew long on Shabbat afternoon. You have given me a gift of immeasurable beauty and depth. I will always be grateful as I try to follow your example. This book is dedicated to you with love and admiration.

Eitan Fishbane

Notes

Introduction

1. See *Mekhilta, Parashat Ki Tisa*, on the phrase *ki 'ani YHVH mekaddishkhem*.

2. This juxtaposition of physical and spiritual sight was developed by the medieval Hebrew poet and philosopher Yehudah ha-Levi. The encounter with Divinity was, for ha-Levi, located in the *'ein ha-lev*—the eye of the heart—which for medieval philosophers meant the vision of the inner mind, the faculty of imagination within the person. *Lev* was a term used for "mind" in medieval Hebrew. The nuances of spiritual sight, and the larger topic of visual experience in Jewish mystical and philosophical sources, have been developed in great depth by Elliot R. Wolfson in his *Through a Speculum That Shines: Vision and Imagination in Medieval Jewish Mysticism* (Princeton, N.J.: Princeton University Press, 1994). For Wolfson's analysis of this phenomenon in the thought of ha-Levi, see pp. 163–87 in that volume.

3. Rabbi Natan states this explicitly in the opening lines of his introduction to *Likutei Tefilot*.

4. For an extensive scholarly treatment of R. Tzadok's thought, including reflections on his approach to the meaning of Shabbat, see Alan Brill, *Thinking God: The Mysticism of Rabbi Zadok of Lublin* (Jersey City, N.J.: Yeshiva University Press, 2002).

5. For nuanced scholarly examinations of this theme in the *Sefat 'Emet*, see Michael Fishbane, "Transcendental Consciousness and Stillness in the Mystical Theology of R. Yehudah Arieh Leib of Gur," in *Sabbath: Idea, History, Reality*, ed. Gerald Blidstein (Be'er Sheva, Israel: Ben Gurion University of the Negev Press, 2004), pp. 119–29; and Yoram Jacobson, "Sanctification of the Ordinary in Gerer Hasidism: The Idea of the Sabbath in the Teachings of the *Sefat 'Emet*" [in Hebrew], in *Tzadikim*

ve-Anshei Ma'aseh: Studies in Polish Hasidism, ed. Rachel Elior, Israel Bartal, and Chone Shmeruk (Jerusalem: Mosad Bialik, 1994), pp. 241–77.

6. The idea of the inner point in the *Sefat 'Emet* has been studied at length in Arthur Green, *The Language of Truth: The Torah Commentary of the Sefat Emet* (Philadelphia: Jewish Publication Society, 1998), pp. xv–xlviii. In a separate essay, Green has also examined the way this motif is shared by Hillel Zeitlin and Abraham Joshua Heschel. See Arthur Green, "Three Warsaw Mystics," in *Kolot Rabbim: The Rivkah Shatz-Uffenheimer Memorial Volume*, vol. 2, ed. Rachel Elior and Joseph Dan (Jerusalem: Hebrew University of Jerusalem Press, 1996), pp. 1–58.

Candle Lighting

1. On the kabbalistic understanding of the prophetic visualization of God, see Elliot R. Wolfson, *Through a Speculum That Shines: Vision and Imagination in Medieval Jewish Mysticism* (Princeton, N.J.: Princeton University Press, 1994).

Wearing White on Shabbat

1. The *Zohar* also poignantly represents the encounter with angels at the commencement of Shabbat. In one striking vignette (*Zohar* 2:136b), the saintly Rabbi Hamnuna Sava is described as emerging from his ritual immersion in the river on the Sabbath eve to behold a vision of the angels ascending and descending between heaven and earth. See the reflections of Elliot K. Ginsburg, *The Sabbath in the Classical Kabbalah* (Albany: State University of New York Press, 1989), p. 248n34; Melila Hellner-Eshed, *A River Flows from Eden: The Language of Mystical Experience in the Zohar*, trans. Nathan Wolski (Stanford, Calif.: Stanford University Press, 2009), pp. 238–39; Daniel Matt, *The Zohar: Pritzker Edition*, vol. 5 (Stanford, Calif.: Stanford University Press, 2009), p. 259.

Soul of the World

1. Abraham Joshua Heschel, *God in Search of Man: A Philosophy of Judaism* (New York: Farrar, Straus and Giroux, 1955).

2. On this question, see Eitan P. Fishbane, "Mystical Contemplation and the Limits of the Mind: The Case of *Sheqel ha-Qodesh*," *The Jewish Quarterly Review* 93:2 (2002): 1–27.

3. On this theme in Jewish mystical literature, see Elliot R. Wolfson, *Through a Speculum That Shines: Vision and Imagination in Medieval Jewish Mysticism* (Princeton, N.J.: Princeton University Press, 1994), 270–78; idem, "Hermeneutics of Light in Medieval Kabbalah" in *The Presence of Light: Divine Radiance and Religious Experience*, ed. M. T. Kapstein (Chicago: University of Chicago Press, 2004), pp. 105–18.

4. For two classic, and opposing, approaches to this problem in the history of Jewish mysticism, see Gershom Scholem, *The Messianic Idea in Judaism and Other Essays* (New York: Schocken Books, 1971), pp. 203–27; and Moshe Idel, *Kabbalah: New Perspectives* (New Haven, Conn.: Yale University Press, 1988), pp. 35–73.

Kiddush

1. The idea of a preexistent spiritual substance called "wisdom" was central to both early Jewish and Christian interpreters of Scripture. In both of these contexts, the preexistent entity was referred to as a word or text—Torah in Jewish midrash and the Logos become Christ in early Christian sources. See the analysis in Daniel Boyarin, *Border Lines: The Partition of Judaeo-Christianity* (Philadelphia: University of Pennsylvania Press, 2004), pp. 89–147, 273–307.

2. The notion that wine leads to new epiphanies of mystical and philosophical insight was also developed by medieval thinkers. See my discussion of this in *As Light Before Dawn: The Inner World of a Medieval Kabbalist* (Stanford, Calif.: Stanford University Press, 2009), pp. 104–107.

3. See *Targum Onkelos* on Genesis 6:2; Rashi also transmits this older tradition in his comments on the verse from Genesis. Also see the comments of Ephraim E. Urbach, *The Sages: The World and Wisdom of the Rabbis of the Talmud*, tran. Israel Abrahams (Cambridge, Mass.: Harvard University Press, 1975), pp. 135–36.

4. See Daniel Abrams, "When Was the Introduction to the *Zohar* Composed?" *Asufot* 8 (1994): 211–226 (in Hebrew).

Eating and Contemplation

1. Leon Kass, *The Hungry Soul: Eating and the Perfecting of Our Nature* (New York: The Free Press, 1994).

Hallah as a Symbol of Spiritual Wholeness

1. On this issue in the thought of Isaac Luria, see the analysis of Lawrence Fine, *Physician of the Soul, Healer of the Cosmos: Isaac Luria and His Kabbalistic Fellowship* (Stanford, Calif.: Stanford University Press, 2003), pp. 135ff. Also see Yoram Jacobson, "The Aspect of the Feminine in Lurianic Kabbalah," in *Gershom Scholem's Major Trends in Jewish Mysticism: 50 Years After*, eds. Peter Schaefer and Joseph Dan (Tübingen, Germany: Mohr Siebeck, 1993), pp. 242–43.

2. On this conception, see the reflections of Gershom Scholem, *The Messianic Idea in Judaism* (New York: Schocken Books, 1971), pp. 1–48; and Moshe Idel, *Messianic Mystics* (New Haven, Conn.: Yale University Press, 2000), pp. 281–83. On the question of *beirur* in the thought of R. Naḥman of Bratzlav, see Chani Haran Smith, *Tuning the Soul: Music as a Spiritual Process in the Thought of Rabbi Naḥman of Bratzlav* (Leiden, The Netherlands: Brill, 2010), pp. 51–54. On its use elsewhere in hasidic thought, see Morris Faierstein, *All Is in the Hands of Heaven: The Teachings of Rabbi Mordecai Joseph Leiner* (Piscataway, N.J.: Gorgias Press, 2005), p. 108.

Refraining from Labor

1. A. J. Heschel, *The Sabbath: Its Meaning for Modern Man* (New York: Farrar, Straus and Giroux, 1951), 67.

The Power of Melody

1. On this question, see the studies of my father and teacher, Michael Fishbane, "Joy and Jewish Spirituality" and "The Mystery of Dance According to Rabbi Naḥman of Bratzlav," in Michael Fishbane, *The Exegetical Imagination: On Jewish Thought and Theology* (Cambridge, Mass.: Harvard University Press, 1998), pp. 151–84, and especially pp. 168–72.

2. On this feature of Bratzlav thought, see the work of Arthur Green, *Tormented Master: The Life and Spiritual Quest of Rabbi Nahman of Bratzlav* (Woodstock, Vt.: Jewish Lights, 1992), originally published by the University of Alabama Press, 1979. This subject is treated extensively by Green, but see specific examples on pp. 107, 122, and 142.

Suggestions for Further Reading

Blidstein, Gerald, ed. *Sabbath: Idea, History, Reality*. Be'er Sheva, Israel: Ben Gurion University of the Negev Press, 2004.

Brill, Alan. *Thinking God: The Mysticism of Rabbi Zadok of Lublin*. Jersey City, N.J.: Yeshiva University Press, 2002.

Buber, Martin. *Hasidism and Modern Man*. New York: Humanities Press International, 1988.

Carlebach, Elisheva. *Palaces of Time: Jewish Calendar and Culture in Early Modern Europe*. Cambridge, Mass.: Belknap Press/Harvard University Press, 2011.

Fine, Lawrence, Eitan Fishbane, and Or N. Rose, eds. *Jewish Mysticism and the Spiritual Life: Classical Texts, Contemporary Reflections*. Woodstock, Vt.: Jewish Lights, 2011.

Fishbane, Michael. *Sacred Attunement: A Jewish Theology*. Chicago: University of Chicago Press, 2008.

Ginsburg, Elliot K. *The Sabbath in the Classical Kabbalah*. Oxford: Littman Library of Jewish Civilization, 2008.

Green, Arthur. *The Language of Truth: The Torah Commentary of the Sefat Emet*. Philadelphia: Jewish Publication Society, 1998.

———. *Tormented Master: The Life and Spiritual Quest of Rabbi Nahman of Bratslav*. Woodstock, Vt.: Jewish Lights, 1992.

Green, Arthur, and Barry W. Holtz, eds., trans. *Your Word Is Fire: The Hasidic Masters on Contemplative Prayer*. Woodstock, Vt.: Jewish Lights, 1993.

Hallamish, Moshe. *Kabbalistic Customs on the Sabbath* [in Hebrew]. Jerusalem: Orḥot Publishers, 2006.

Heschel, Abraham Joshua. *The Sabbath: Its Meaning for Modern Man*. New York: Farrar, Straus and Giroux, 1951. Reprinted with an introduction by Susannah Heschel. New York: Farrar, Straus and Giroux, 2005.

Idel, Moshe. *Hasidism: Between Ecstasy and Magic*. Albany: State University of New York Press, 1995.

Jacobson, Yoram. "Sanctification of the Ordinary in Gerer Hasidism: The Idea of the Sabbath in the Teachings of the *Sefat 'Emet*" [in Hebrew]. In *Tzadikim ve-Anshei Ma'aseh: Studies in Polish Hasidism*, edited by Rachel Elior, Israel Bartal, and Chone Shmeruk, pp. 241–77. Jerusalem: Mosad Bialik, 1994.

Kallus, Menachem. *Pillar of Prayer: Guidance in Contemplative Prayer, Sacred Study, and the Spiritual Life, from the Ba'al Shem Tov and His Circle*. Louisville, Ky., Fons Vitae, 2011.

Kimelman, Reuven. *The Mystical Meaning of Lekhah Dodi and Kabbalat Shabbat* [in Hebrew]. Los Angeles: Cherub Press, 2003.

Kushner, Lawrence, and Nehemia Polen. *Filling Words with Light: Hasidic and Mystical Reflections on Jewish Prayer*. Woodstock, Vt.: Jewish Lights, 2007.

Lamm, Norman. *The Religious Thought of Hasidism: Text and Commentary*. Hoboken, N.J.: Yeshiva University Press, 1999.

Magid, Shaul. *Hasidism on the Margin: Reconciliation, Antinomianism, and Messianism*. Madison: University of Wisconsin Press, 2003.

———. "The Holocaust as Inverted Miracle: Shalom Noah Barzofsky of Slonim on the Divine Nature of Radical Evil." In *Spiritual Authority: Struggles over Cultural Power in Jewish Thought*, edited by Howard Kreisel, Boaz Huss, and Uri Ehrlich, pp. 33–62. Be'er Sheva, Israel: Ben-Gurion University of the Negev, 2009.

Matt, Daniel C. *The Essential Kabbalah: The Heart of Jewish Mysticism*. New York: HarperOne, 1996.

Rose, Or N., and Ebn Leader, eds., trans. *God in All Moments: Mystical and Practical Spiritual Wisdom from Hasidic Masters*. Woodstock, Vt.: Jewish Lights, 2004.

Schatz-Uffenheimer, Rivka. *Hasidism as Mysticism: Quietistic Elements in Eighteenth-Century Hasidic Thought*. Translated from the Hebrew by Jonathan Chipman. Princeton, N.J., and Jerusalem: Princeton University Press/Magnes Press, 1993.

Shapiro, Rami. *Tanya, the Masterpiece of Hasidic Wisdom: Selections Annotated & Explained*. Woodstock, Vt.: SkyLight Paths, 2010.

Shulevitz, Judith. *The Sabbath World: Glimpses of a Different Order of Time*. New York: Random House, 2010.

Tishby, Isaiah. *The Wisdom of the Zohar*. Vol. 3. Oxford: Littman Library of Jewish Civilization, 1989.

Wolfson, Elliot R. *Alef, Mem, Tau: Kabbalistic Musings on Time, Truth, and Death*. Berkeley: University of California Press, 2006.

Bar/Bat Mitzvah

The Mitzvah Project Book
Making Mitzvah Part of Your Bar/Bat Mitzvah ... and Your Life
By Liz Suneby and Diane Heiman; Foreword by Rabbi Jeffrey K. Salkin; Preface by Rabbi Sharon Brous
The go-to source for Jewish young adults and their families looking to make the
world a better place through good deeds—big or small.
6 x 9, 224 pp, Quality PB Original, 978-1-58023-458-0 **$16.99** *For ages 11–13*

The JGirl's Guide: The Young Jewish Woman's Handbook for Coming of Age
By Penina Adelman, Ali Feldman and Shulamit Reinharz
6 x 9, 240 pp, Quality PB, 978-1-58023-215-9 **$14.99** *For ages 11 & up*

The JGirl's Teacher's and Parent's Guide 8½ x 11, 56 pp, PB, 978-1-58023-225-8 **$8.99**

The Bar/Bat Mitzvah Memory Book, 2nd Edition: An Album for Treasuring the
Spiritual Celebration *By Rabbi Jeffrey K. Salkin and Nina Salkin*
8 x 10, 48 pp, 2-color text, Deluxe HC, ribbon marker, 978-1-58023-263-0 **$19.99**

For Kids—Putting God on Your Guest List, 2nd Edition: How to Claim the
Spiritual Meaning of Your Bar or Bat Mitzvah *By Rabbi Jeffrey K. Salkin*
6 x 9, 144 pp, Quality PB, 978-1-58023-308-8 **$15.99** *For ages 11–13*

Putting God on the Guest List, 3rd Edition: How to Reclaim the Spiritual
Meaning of Your Child's Bar or Bat Mitzvah *By Rabbi Jeffrey K. Salkin*
6 x 9, 224 pp, Quality PB, 978-1-58023-222-7 **$16.99**; HC, 978-1-58023-260-9 **$24.99**

Putting God on the Guest List Teacher's Guide
8½ x 11, 48 pp, PB, 978-1-58023-226-5 **$8.99**

Tough Questions Jews Ask, 2nd Edition: A Young Adult's Guide to Building a Jewish Life
By Rabbi Edward Feinstein 6 x 9, 160 pp, Quality PB, 978-1-58023-454-2 **$16.99** *For ages 11 & up*

Tough Questions Jews Ask Teacher's Guide 8½ x 11, 72 pp, PB, 978-1-58023-187-9 **$8.95**

Bible Study/Midrash

Sage Tales: Wisdom and Wonder from the Rabbis of the Talmud
By Rabbi Burton L Visotzky Illustrates how the stories of the Rabbis who lived in the
first generations following the destruction of the Jerusalem Temple illuminate
modern life's most pressing issues. 6 x 9, 256 pp, HC, 978-1-58023-456-6 **$24.99**

The Modern Men's Torah Commentary: New Insights from Jewish Men on the
54 Weekly Torah Portions *Edited by Rabbi Jeffrey K. Salkin*
6 x 9, 368 pp, HC, 978-1-58023-395-8 **$24.99**

The Genesis of Leadership: What the Bible Teaches Us about Vision, Values and
Leading Change *By Rabbi Nathan Laufer; Foreword by Senator Joseph I. Lieberman*
6 x 9, 288 pp, Quality PB, 978-1-58023-352-1 **$18.99**

Hineini in Our Lives: Learning How to Respond to Others through 14 Biblical Texts and
Personal Stories *By Rabbi Norman J. Cohen, PhD* 6 x 9, 240 pp, Quality PB, 978-1-58023-274-6 **$16.99**

A Man's Responsibility: A Jewish Guide to Being a Son, a Partner in Marriage, a Father and a
Community Leader *By Rabbi Joseph B. Meszler* 6 x 9, 192 pp, Quality PB, 978-1-58023-435-1 **$16.99**

Moses and the Journey to Leadership: Timeless Lessons of Effective Management from
the Bible and Today's Leaders *By Rabbi Norman J. Cohen, PhD*
6 x 9, 240 pp, Quality PB, 978-1-58023-351-4 **$18.99**; HC, 978-1-58023-227-2 **$21.99**

Righteous Gentiles in the Hebrew Bible: Ancient Role Models for Sacred Relationships
By Rabbi Jeffrey K. Salkin; Foreword by Rabbi Harold M. Schulweis;
Preface by Phyllis Tickle 6 x 9, 192 pp, Quality PB, 978-1-58023-364-4 **$18.99**

The Wisdom of Judaism: An Introduction to the Values of the Talmud
By Rabbi Dov Peretz Elkins 6 x 9, 192 pp, Quality PB, 978-1-58023-327-9 **$16.99**

Meditation

Jewish Meditation Practices for Everyday Life
Awakening Your Heart, Connecting with God
By Rabbi Jeff Roth
Offers a fresh take on meditation that draws on life experience and living life with greater clarity as opposed to the traditional method of rigorous study.
6 x 9, 224 pp, Quality PB, 978-1-58023-397-2 **$18.99**

The Handbook of Jewish Meditation Practices
A Guide for Enriching the Sabbath and Other Days of Your Life
By Rabbi David A. Cooper Easy-to-learn meditation techniques.
6 x 9, 208 pp, Quality PB, 978-1-58023-102-2 **$16.95**

Discovering Jewish Meditation, 2nd Edition
Instruction & Guidance for Learning an Ancient Spiritual Practice
By Nan Fink Gefen, PhD 6 x 9, 208 pp, Quality PB, 978-1-58023-462-7 **$16.99**

Meditation from the Heart of Judaism
Today's Teachers Share Their Practices, Techniques, and Faith
Edited by Avram Davis 6 x 9, 256 pp, Quality PB, 978-1-58023-049-0 **$16.95**

Ritual/Sacred Practices

The Jewish Dream Book: The Key to Opening the Inner Meaning of Your Dreams
By Vanessa L. Ochs, PhD, with Elizabeth Ochs; Illus. by Kristina Swarner
Instructions for how modern people can perform ancient Jewish dream practices and dream interpretations drawn from the Jewish wisdom tradition.
8 x 8, 128 pp, Full-color illus., Deluxe PB w/ flaps, 978-1-58023-132-9 **$16.95**

God in Your Body: Kabbalah, Mindfulness and Embodied Spiritual Practice
By Jay Michaelson
The first comprehensive treatment of the body in Jewish spiritual practice and an essential guide to the sacred.
6 x 9, 272 pp, Quality PB, 978-1-58023-304-0 **$18.99**

The Book of Jewish Sacred Practices: CLAL's Guide to Everyday & Holiday Rituals & Blessings
Edited by Rabbi Irwin Kula and Vanessa L. Ochs, PhD
6 x 9, 368 pp, Quality PB, 978-1-58023-152-7 **$18.95**

Jewish Ritual: A Brief Introduction for Christians
By Rabbi Kerry M. Olitzky and Rabbi Daniel Judson
5½ x 8½, 144 pp, Quality PB, 978-1-58023-210-4 **$14.99**

The Rituals & Practices of a Jewish Life: A Handbook for Personal Spiritual Renewal
Edited by Rabbi Kerry M. Olitzky and Rabbi Daniel Judson
6 x 9, 272 pp, Illus., Quality PB, 978-1-58023-169-5 **$18.95**

The Sacred Art of Lovingkindness: Preparing to Practice
By Rabbi Rami Shapiro 5½ x 8½, 176 pp, Quality PB, 978-1-59473-151-8 **$16.99**
(A book from SkyLight Paths, Jewish Lights' sister imprint)

Science Fiction/Mystery & Detective Fiction

Criminal Kabbalah: An Intriguing Anthology of Jewish Mystery & Detective Fiction
Edited by Lawrence W. Raphael; Foreword by Laurie R. King
All-new stories from twelve of today's masters of mystery and detective fiction—sure to delight mystery buffs of all faith traditions.
6 x 9, 256 pp, Quality PB, 978-1-58023-109-1 **$16.95**

Mystery Midrash: An Anthology of Jewish Mystery & Detective Fiction
Edited by Lawrence W. Raphael; Preface by Joel Siegel
6 x 9, 304 pp, Quality PB, 978-1-58023-055-1 **$16.95**

Wandering Stars: An Anthology of Jewish Fantasy & Science Fiction
Edited by Jack Dann; Introduction by Isaac Asimov
6 x 9, 272 pp, Quality PB, 978-1-58023-005-6 **$18.99**

More Wandering Stars: An Anthology of Outstanding Stories of Jewish Fantasy and Science Fiction
Edited by Jack Dann; Introduction by Isaac Asimov
6 x 9, 192 pp, Quality PB, 978-1-58023-063-6 **$16.95**

Holidays/Holy Days

Who by Fire, Who by Water—Un'taneh Tokef
Edited by Rabbi Lawrence A. Hoffman, PhD
Examines the prayer's theology, authorship and poetry through a set of lively essays, all written in accessible language.
6 x 9, 272 pp, HC, 978-1-58023-424-5 **$24.99**

All These Vows—Kol Nidre
Edited by Rabbi Lawrence A. Hoffman, PhD
The most memorable prayer of the Jewish New Year—what it means, why we sing it, and the secret of its magical appeal.
6 x 9, 288 pp, HC, 978-1-58023-430-6 **$24.99**

Rosh Hashanah Readings: Inspiration, Information and Contemplation
Yom Kippur Readings: Inspiration, Information and Contemplation
Edited by Rabbi Dov Peretz Elkins; Section Introductions from Arthur Green's These Are the Words
Rosh Hashanah: 6 x 9, 400 pp, Quality PB, 978-1-58023-437-5 **$19.99**; HC, 978-1-58023-239-5 **$24.99**
Yom Kippur: 6 x 9, 368 pp, Quality PB, 978-1-58023-438-2 **$19.99**; HC, 978-1-58023-271-5 **$24.99**

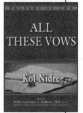

Jewish Holidays: A Brief Introduction for Christians
By Rabbi Kerry M. Olitzky and Rabbi Daniel Judson
5½ x 8½, 176 pp, Quality PB, 978-1-58023-302-6 **$16.99**

Reclaiming Judaism as a Spiritual Practice: Holy Days and Shabbat
By Rabbi Goldie Milgram 7 x 9, 272 pp, Quality PB, 978-1-58023-205-0 **$19.99**

Shabbat, 2nd Edition: The Family Guide to Preparing for and Celebrating the Sabbath
By Dr. Ron Wolfson 7 x 9, 320 pp, Illus., Quality PB, 978-1-58023-164-0 **$19.99**

Hanukkah, 2nd Edition: The Family Guide to Spiritual Celebration
By Dr. Ron Wolfson 7 x 9, 240 pp, Illus., Quality PB, 978-1-58023-122-0 **$18.95**

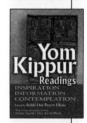

The Jewish Family Fun Book, 2nd Edition
Holiday Projects, Everyday Activities, and Travel Ideas with Jewish Themes
By Danielle Dardashti and Roni Sarig; Illus. by Avi Katz
6 x 9, 304 pp, 70+ b/w illus. & diagrams, Quality PB, 978-1-58023-333-0 **$18.99**

Passover

My People's Passover Haggadah
Traditional Texts, Modern Commentaries
Edited by Rabbi Lawrence A. Hoffman, PhD, and David Arnow, PhD
A diverse and exciting collection of commentaries on the traditional Passover Haggadah—in two volumes!
Vol. 1: 7 x 10, 304 pp, HC, 978-1-58023-354-5 **$24.99**
Vol. 2: 7 x 10, 320 pp, HC, 978-1-58023-346-0 **$24.99**

Freedom Journeys: The Tale of Exodus and Wilderness across Millennia
By Rabbi Arthur O. Waskow and Rabbi Phyllis O. Berman
Explores how the story of Exodus echoes in our own time, calling us to relearn and rethink the Passover story through social-justice, ecological, feminist and interfaith perspectives. 6 x 9, 288 pp, HC, 978-1-58023-445-0 **$24.99**

Leading the Passover Journey: The Seder's Meaning Revealed,
the Haggadah's Story Retold *By Rabbi Nathan Laufer*
Uncovers the hidden meaning of the Seder's rituals and customs.
6 x 9, 224 pp, Quality PB, 978-1-58023-399-6 **$18.99**; HC, 978-1-58023-211-1 **$24.99**

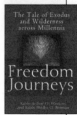

Creating Lively Passover Seders, 2nd Edition: A Sourcebook of Engaging Tales,
Texts & Activities *By David Arnow, PhD* 7 x 9, 464 pp, Quality PB, 978-1-58023-444-3 **$24.99**

Passover, 2nd Edition: The Family Guide to Spiritual Celebration
By Dr. Ron Wolfson with Joel Lurie Grishaver 7 x 9, 416 pp, Quality PB, 978-1-58023-174-9 **$19.95**

The Women's Passover Companion: Women's Reflections on the Festival of Freedom
Edited by Rabbi Sharon Cohen Anisfeld, Tara Mohr and Catherine Spector; Foreword by Paula E. Hyman
6 x 9, 352 pp, Quality PB, 978-1-58023-231-9 **$19.99**; HC, 978-1-58023-128-2 **$24.95**

The Women's Seder Sourcebook: Rituals & Readings for Use at the Passover Seder
Edited by Rabbi Sharon Cohen Anisfeld, Tara Mohr and Catherine Spector
6 x 9, 384 pp, Quality PB, 978-1-58023-232-6 **$19.99**

Ecology/Environment

A Wild Faith: Jewish Ways into Wilderness, Wilderness Ways into Judaism
By Rabbi Mike Comins; Foreword by Nigel Savage 6 x 9, 240 pp, Quality PB, 978-1-58023-316-3 **$16.99**

Ecology & the Jewish Spirit: Where Nature & the Sacred Meet
Edited by Ellen Bernstein 6 x 9, 288 pp, Quality PB, 978-1-58023-082-7 **$18.99**

Torah of the Earth: Exploring 4,000 Years of Ecology in Jewish Thought
Vol. 1: Biblical Israel & Rabbinic Judaism; Vol. 2: Zionism & Eco-Judaism
Edited by Rabbi Arthur Waskow Vol. 1: 6 x 9, 272 pp, Quality PB, 978-1-58023-086-5 **$19.95**
Vol. 2: 6 x 9, 336 pp, Quality PB, 978-1-58023-087-2 **$19.95**

The Way Into Judaism and the Environment *By Jeremy Benstein, PhD*
6 x 9, 288 pp, Quality PB, 978-1-58023-368-2 **$18.99**; HC, 978-1-58023-268-5 **$24.99**

Graphic Novels/History

The Adventures of Rabbi Harvey: A Graphic Novel of Jewish Wisdom and Wit in the
Wild West *By Steve Sheinkin* 6 x 9, 144 pp, Full-color illus., Quality PB, 978-1-58023-310-1 **$16.99**

Rabbi Harvey Rides Again: A Graphic Novel of Jewish Folktales Let Loose in the
Wild West *By Steve Sheinkin* 6 x 9, 144 pp, Full-color illus., Quality PB, 978-1-58023-347-7 **$16.99**

Rabbi Harvey vs. the Wisdom Kid: A Graphic Novel of Dueling
Jewish Folktales in the Wild West *By Steve Sheinkin*
Rabbi Harvey's first book-length adventure—and toughest challenge.
6 x 9, 144 pp, Full-color illus., Quality PB, 978-1-58023-422-1 **$16.99**

The Story of the Jews: A 4,000-Year Adventure—A Graphic History Book
By Stan Mack 6 x 9, 288 pp, Illus., Quality PB, 978-1-58023-155-8 **$16.99**

Grief/Healing

Facing Illness, Finding God: How Judaism Can Help You and Caregivers
Cope When Body or Spirit Fails *By Rabbi Joseph B. Meszler*
Will help you find spiritual strength for healing amid the fear, pain and chaos of
illness. 6 x 9, 208 pp, Quality PB, 978-1-58023-423-8 **$16.99**

Midrash & Medicine: Healing Body and Soul in the Jewish Interpretive
Tradition *Edited by Rabbi William Cutter, PhD; Foreword by Michele F. Prince, LCSW, MAJCS*
Explores how midrash can help you see beyond the physical aspects of healing to
tune in to your spiritual source.
6 x 9, 352 pp, Quality PB, 978-1-58023-484-9 **$21.99**; HC, 978-1-58023-428-3 **$29.99**

Healing from Despair: Choosing Wholeness in a Broken World
By Rabbi Elie Kaplan Spitz with Erica Shapiro Taylor; Foreword by Abraham J. Twerski, MD
5½ x 8½, 208 pp, Quality PB, 978-1-58023-436-8 **$16.99**

Healing and the Jewish Imagination: Spiritual and Practical Perspectives on
Judaism and Health *Edited by Rabbi William Cutter, PhD*
6 x 9, 240 pp, Quality PB, 978-1-58023-373-6 **$19.99**

Grief in Our Seasons: A Mourner's Kaddish Companion *By Rabbi Kerry M. Olitzky*
4½ x 6½, 448 pp, Quality PB, 978-1-879045-55-2 **$15.95**

Healing of Soul, Healing of Body: Spiritual Leaders Unfold the Strength & Solace
in Psalms *Edited by Rabbi Simkha Y. Weintraub, LCSW*
6 x 9, 128 pp, 2-color illus. text, Quality PB, 978-1-879045-31-6 **$16.99**

Mourning & Mitzvah, 2nd Edition: A Guided Journal for Walking the Mourner's
Path through Grief to Healing *By Rabbi Anne Brener, LCSW*
7½ x 9, 304 pp, Quality PB, 978-1-58023-113-8 **$19.99**

Tears of Sorrow, Seeds of Hope, 2nd Edition: A Jewish Spiritual Companion for
Infertility and Pregnancy Loss *By Rabbi Nina Beth Cardin*
6 x 9, 208 pp, Quality PB, 978-1-58023-233-3 **$18.99**

A Time to Mourn, a Time to Comfort, 2nd Edition: A Guide to Jewish
Bereavement *By Dr. Ron Wolfson; Foreword by Rabbi David J. Wolpe*
7 x 9, 384 pp, Quality PB, 978-1-58023-253-1 **$21.99**

When a Grandparent Dies: A Kid's Own Remembering Workbook for Dealing
with Shiva and the Year Beyond *By Nechama Liss-Levinson, PhD*
8 x 10, 48 pp, 2-color text, HC, 978-1-879045-44-6 **$15.95** *For ages 7–13*

Congregation Resources

Empowered Judaism: What Independent Minyanim Can Teach Us about Building Vibrant Jewish Communities
By Rabbi Elie Kaunfer; Foreword by Prof. Jonathan D. Sarna
Examines the independent minyan movement and the lessons these grassroots communities can provide. 6 x 9, 224 pp, Quality PB, 978-1-58023-412-2 **$18.99**

Spiritual Boredom: Rediscovering the Wonder of Judaism *By Dr. Erica Brown*
Breaks through the surface of spiritual boredom to find the reservoir of meaning within. 6 x 9, 208 pp, HC, 978-1-58023-405-4 **$21.99**

Building a Successful Volunteer Culture
Finding Meaning in Service in the Jewish Community
By Rabbi Charles Simon; Foreword by Shelley Lindauer; Preface by Dr. Ron Wolfson
Shows you how to develop and maintain the volunteers who are essential to the vitality of your organization and community. 6 x 9, 192 pp, Quality PB, 978-1-58023-408-5 **$16.99**

The Case for Jewish Peoplehood: Can We Be One?
By Dr. Erica Brown and Dr. Misha Galperin; Foreword by Rabbi Joseph Telushkin
6 x 9, 224 pp, HC, 978-1-58023-401-6 **$21.99**

Inspired Jewish Leadership: Practical Approaches to Building Strong Communities
By Dr. Erica Brown 6 x 9, 256 pp, HC, 978-1-58023-361-3 **$27.99**

Jewish Pastoral Care, 2nd Edition: A Practical Handbook from Traditional & Contemporary Sources *Edited by Rabbi Dayle A. Friedman, MSW, MAJCS, BCC*
6 x 9, 528 pp, Quality PB, 978-1-58023-427-6 **$30.00**

Rethinking Synagogues: A New Vocabulary for Congregational Life
By Rabbi Lawrence A. Hoffman, PhD 6 x 9, 240 pp, Quality PB, 978-1-58023-248-7 **$19.99**

The Spirituality of Welcoming: How to Transform Your Congregation into a Sacred Community *By Dr. Ron Wolfson* 6 x 9, 224 pp, Quality PB, 978-1-58023-244-9 **$19.99**

Children's Books

Around the World in One Shabbat
Jewish People Celebrate the Sabbath Together
By Durga Yael Bernhard
Takes your child on a colorful adventure to share the many ways Jewish people celebrate Shabbat around the world.
11 x 8½, 32 pp, Full-color illus., HC, 978-1-58023-433-7 **$18.99** *For ages 3–6*

What You Will See Inside a Synagogue
By Rabbi Lawrence A. Hoffman, PhD, and Dr. Ron Wolfson; Full-color photos by Bill Aron
A colorful, fun-to-read introduction that explains the ways and whys of Jewish worship and religious life.
8½ x 10½, 32 pp, Full-color photos, Quality PB, 978-1-59473-256-0 **$8.99** *For ages 6 & up*
(A book from SkyLight Paths, Jewish Lights' sister imprint)

Because Nothing Looks Like God
By Lawrence Kushner and Karen Kushner Introduces children to the possibilities of spiritual life. 11 x 8½, 32 pp, Full-color illus., HC, 978-1-58023-092-6 **$17.99** *For ages 4 & up*

The Book of Miracles: A Young Person's Guide to Jewish Spiritual Awareness
Written and illus. by Lawrence Kushner
6 x 9, 96 pp, 2-color illus., HC, 978-1-879045-78-1 **$16.95** *For ages 9–13*

In God's Hands *By Lawrence Kushner and Gary Schmidt* 9 x 12, 32 pp, Full-color illus., HC, 978-1-58023-224-1 **$16.99** *For ages 5 & up*

In Our Image: God's First Creatures *By Nancy Sohn Swartz*
9 x 12, 32 pp, Full-color illus., HC, 978-1-879045-99-6 **$16.95** *For ages 4 & up*

The Kids' Fun Book of Jewish Time
By Emily Sper 9 x 7½, 24 pp, Full-color illus., HC, 978-1-58023-311-8 **$16.99** *For ages 3–6*

What Makes Someone a Jew? *By Lauren Seidman*
Reflects the changing face of American Judaism.
10 x 8½, 32 pp, Full-color photos, Quality PB, 978-1-58023-321-7 **$8.99** *For ages 3–6*

Children's Books by Sandy Eisenberg Sasso

Adam & Eve's First Sunset: God's New Day
Explores fear and hope, faith and gratitude in ways that will delight kids and adults—inspiring us to bless each of God's days and nights.
9 x 12, 32 pp, Full-color illus., HC, 978-1-58023-177-0 **$17.95** *For ages 4 & up*

Also Available as a Board Book: **Adam and Eve's New Day**
5 x 5, 24 pp, Full-color illus., Board Book, 978-1-59473-205-8 **$7.99** *For ages 0–4*
(A book from SkyLight Paths, Jewish Lights' sister imprint)

But God Remembered: Stories of Women from Creation to the Promised Land
Four different stories of women—Lilith, Serach, Bityah and the Daughters of Z—teach us important values through their faith and actions.
9 x 12, 32 pp, Full-color illus., Quality PB, 978-1-58023-372-9 **$8.99** *For ages 8 & up*

Cain & Abel: Finding the Fruits of Peace
Shows children that we have the power to deal with anger in positive ways. Provides questions for kids and adults to explore together.
9 x 12, 32 pp, Full-color illus., HC, 978-1-58023-123-7 **$16.95** *For ages 5 & up*

For Heaven's Sake
Heaven is often found where you least expect it.
9 x 12, 32 pp, Full-color illus., HC, 978-1-58023-054-4 **$16.95** *For ages 4 & up*

God in Between
If you wanted to find God, where would you look? This magical, mythical tale teaches that God can be found where we are: within all of us and the relationships between us. 9 x 12, 32 pp, Full-color illus., HC, 978-1-879045-86-6 **$16.95** *For ages 4 & up*

God Said Amen
An inspiring story about hearing the answers to our prayers.
9 x 12, 32 pp, Full-color illus., HC, 978-1-58023-080-3 **$16.95** *For ages 4 & up*

God's Paintbrush: Special 10th Anniversary Edition
Wonderfully interactive, invites children of all faiths and backgrounds to encounter God through moments in their own lives. Provides questions adult and child can explore together. 11 x 8½, 32 pp, Full-color illus., HC, 978-1-58023-195-4 **$17.95** *For ages 4 & up*

Also Available as a Board Book: **I Am God's Paintbrush**
5 x 5, 24 pp, Full-color illus., Board Book, 978-1-59473-265-2 **$7.99** *For ages 0–4*
(A book from SkyLight Paths, Jewish Lights' sister imprint)

Also Available: **God's Paintbrush Teacher's Guide**
8½ x 11, 32 pp, PB, 978-1-879045-57-6 **$8.95**

God's Paintbrush Celebration Kit
A Spiritual Activity Kit for Teachers and Students of All Faiths, All Backgrounds
9½ x 12, 40 Full-color Activity Sheets & Teacher Folder w/ complete instructions
HC, 978-1-58023-050-6 **$21.95**
8-Student Activity Sheet Pack (40 sheets/5 sessions), 978-1-58023-058-2 **$19.95**

In God's Name
Like an ancient myth in its poetic text and vibrant illustrations, this award-winning modern fable about the search for God's name celebrates the diversity and, at the same time, the unity of all people.
9 x 12, 32 pp, Full-color illus., HC, 978-1-879045-26-2 **$16.99** *For ages 4 & up*

Also Available as a Board Book: **What Is God's Name?**
5 x 5, 24 pp, Full-color illus., Board Book, 978-1-893361-10-2 **$7.99** *For ages 0–4*
(A book from SkyLight Paths, Jewish Lights' sister imprint)

Also Available in Spanish: **El nombre de Dios**
9 x 12, 32 pp, Full-color illus., HC, 978-1-893361-63-8 **$16.95** *For ages 4 & up*

Noah's Wife: The Story of Naamah
When God tells Noah to bring the animals of the world onto the ark, God also calls on Naamah, Noah's wife, to save each plant on Earth. Based on an ancient text.
9 x 12, 32 pp, Full-color illus., HC, 978-1-58023-134-3 **$16.95** *For ages 4 & up*

Also Available as a Board Book: **Naamah, Noah's Wife**
5 x 5, 24 pp, Full-color illus., Board Book, 978-1-893361-56-0 **$7.95** *For ages 0–4*
(A book from SkyLight Paths, Jewish Lights' sister imprint)

Spirituality/Crafts

Jewish Threads: Hands-On Guide to Stitching Spiritual Intention into Jewish Fabric Crafts *By Diana Drew with Robert Grayson*
Learn how to make your own Jewish fabric crafts with spiritual intention—a journey of creativity, imagination and inspiration. Thirty projects.
7 x 9, 288 pp, 8-page color insert, b/w illus., Quality PB Original, 978-1-58023-442-9 **$19.99**

(from SkyLight Paths, Jewish Lights' sister imprint)

Beading—The Creative Spirit: Finding Your Sacred Center through the Art of Beadwork *By Wendy Ellsworth*
Invites you on a spiritual pilgrimage into the kaleidoscope world of glass and color.
7 x 9, 240 pp, 8-page full-color insert, b/w photos and diagrams, Quality PB, 978-1-59473-267-6 **$18.99**

Contemplative Crochet: A Hands-On Guide for Interlocking Faith and Craft *By Cindy Crandall-Frazier; Foreword by Linda Skolnik*
Will take you on a path deeper into your crocheting and your spiritual awareness.
7 x 9, 208 pp, b/w photos, Quality PB, 978-1-59473-238-6 **$16.99**

The Knitting Way: A Guide to Spiritual Self-Discovery
By Linda Skolnik and Janice MacDaniels
Shows how to use knitting to strengthen your spiritual self.
7 x 9, 240 pp, b/w photos, Quality PB, 978-1-59473-079-5 **$16.99**

The Painting Path: Embodying Spiritual Discovery through Yoga, Brush and Color *By Linda Novick; Foreword by Richard Segalman*
Explores the divine connection you can experience through art.
7 x 9, 208 pp, 8-page full-color insert, b/w photos, Quality PB, 978-1-59473-226-3 **$18.99**

The Quilting Path: A Guide to Spiritual Self-Discovery through Fabric, Thread and Kabbalah *By Louise Silk* Explores how to cultivate personal growth through quilt making. 7 x 9, 192 pp, b/w photos, Quality PB, 978-1-59473-206-5 **$16.99**

The Scrapbooking Journey: A Hands-On Guide to Spiritual Discovery
By Cory Richardson-Lauve; Foreword by Stacy Julian
Reveals how this craft can become a practice used to deepen and shape your life.
7 x 9, 176 pp, 8-page full-color insert, b/w photos, Quality PB, 978-1-59473-216-4 **$18.99**

Travel

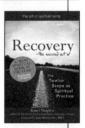

Israel—A Spiritual Travel Guide, 2nd Edition: A Companion for the Modern Jewish Pilgrim *By Rabbi Lawrence A. Hoffman, PhD*
Helps today's pilgrim tap into the deep spiritual meaning of the ancient—and modern—sites of the Holy Land.
4¾ x 10, 256 pp, Illus., Quality PB, 978-1-58023-261-6 **$18.99**

Also Available: **The Israel Mission Leader's Guide** 5½ x 8½, 16 pp, PB, 978-1-58023-085-8 **$4.95**

Twelve Steps

Recovery—The Sacred Art: The Twelve Steps as Spiritual Practice
By Rami Shapiro; Foreword by Joan Borysenko, PhD
Draws on insights and practices of different religious traditions to help you move more deeply into the universal spirituality of the Twelve Step system.
5½ x 8½, 240 pp, Quality PB Original, 978-1-59473-259-1 **$16.99**
(A book from SkyLight Paths, Jewish Lights' sister imprint)

100 Blessings Every Day: Daily Twelve Step Recovery Affirmations, Exercises for Personal Growth & Renewal Reflecting Seasons of the Jewish Year *By Rabbi Kerry M. Olitzky; Foreword by Rabbi Neil Gillman, PhD* 4½ x 6½, 432 pp, Quality PB, 978-1-879045-30-9 **$16.99**

Recovery from Codependence: A Jewish Twelve Steps Guide to Healing Your Soul
By Rabbi Kerry M. Olitzky 6 x 9, 160 pp, Quality PB, 978-1-879045-32-3 **$13.95**

Twelve Jewish Steps to Recovery, 2nd Edition: A Personal Guide to Turning from Alcoholism & Other Addictions—Drugs, Food, Gambling, Sex ...
By Rabbi Kerry M. Olitzky and Stuart A. Copans, MD; Preface by Abraham J. Twerski, MD
6 x 9, 160 pp, Quality PB, 978-1-58023-409-2 **$16.99**

Theology/Philosophy/The Way Into... Series

The Way Into... series offers an accessible and highly usable "guided tour" of the Jewish faith, people, history and beliefs—in total, an introduction to Judaism that will enable you to understand and interact with the sacred texts of the Jewish tradition. Each volume is written by a leading contemporary scholar and teacher, and explores one key aspect of Judaism. The Way Into... series enables all readers to achieve a real sense of Jewish cultural literacy through guided study.

The Way Into Encountering God in Judaism
By Rabbi Neil Gillman, PhD
For everyone who wants to understand how Jews have encountered God throughout history and today.
6 x 9, 240 pp, Quality PB, 978-1-58023-199-2 **$18.99**; HC, 978-1-58023-025-4 **$21.95**
Also Available: **The Jewish Approach to God:** A Brief Introduction for Christians
By Rabbi Neil Gillman, PhD
5½ x 8½, 192 pp, Quality PB, 978-1-58023-190-9 **$16.95**

The Way Into Jewish Mystical Tradition
By Rabbi Lawrence Kushner
Allows readers to interact directly with the sacred mystical texts of the Jewish tradition. An accessible introduction to the concepts of Jewish mysticism, their religious and spiritual significance, and how they relate to life today.
6 x 9, 224 pp, Quality PB, 978-1-58023-200-5 **$18.99**; HC, 978-1-58023-029-2 **$21.95**

The Way Into Jewish Prayer
By Rabbi Lawrence A. Hoffman, PhD
Opens the door to 3,000 years of Jewish prayer, making anyone feel at home in the Jewish way of communicating with God.
6 x 9, 208 pp, Quality PB, 978-1-58023-201-2 **$18.99**

The Way Into Jewish Prayer Teacher's Guide
By Rabbi Jennifer Ossakow Goldsmith
8½ x 11, 42 pp, PB, 978-1-58023-345-3 **$8.99**
Download a free copy at www.jewishlights.com.

The Way Into Judaism and the Environment
By Jeremy Benstein, PhD
Explores the ways in which Judaism contributes to contemporary social-environmental issues, the extent to which Judaism is part of the problem and how it can be part of the solution.
6 x 9, 288 pp, Quality PB, 978-1-58023-368-2 **$18.99**

The Way Into *Tikkun Olam* (Repairing the World)
By Rabbi Elliot N. Dorff, PhD
An accessible introduction to the Jewish concept of the individual's responsibility to care for others and repair the world.
6 x 9, 304 pp, Quality PB, 978-1-58023-328-6 **$18.99**

The Way Into Torah
By Rabbi Norman J. Cohen, PhD
Helps guide you in the exploration of the origins and development of Torah, explains why it should be studied and how to do it.
6 x 9, 176 pp, Quality PB, 978-1-58023-198-5 **$16.99**

The Way Into the Varieties of Jewishness
By Sylvia Barack Fishman, PhD
Explores the religious and historical understanding of what it has meant to be Jewish from ancient times to the present controversy over "Who is a Jew?"
6 x 9, 288 pp, Quality PB, 978-1-58023-367-5 **$18.99**; HC, 978-1-58023-030-8 **$24.99**

Theology/Philosophy

The God Who Hates Lies: Confronting & Rethinking Jewish Tradition
By Dr. David Hartman with Charlie Buckholtz
The world's leading Modern Orthodox Jewish theologian probes the deepest questions at the heart of what it means to be a human being and a Jew.
6 x 9, 208 pp, HC, 978-1-58023-455-9 **$24.99**

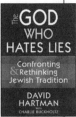

Jewish Theology in Our Time: A New Generation Explores the Foundations and Future of Jewish Belief *Edited by Rabbi Elliot J. Cosgrove, PhD; Foreword by Rabbi David J. Wolpe; Preface by Rabbi Carole B. Balin, PhD*
A powerful and challenging examination of what Jews can believe—by a new generation's most dynamic and innovative thinkers.
6 x 9, 240 pp, HC, 978-1-58023-413-9 **$24.99**

Maimonides, Spinoza and Us: Toward an Intellectually Vibrant Judaism
By Rabbi Marc D. Angel, PhD A challenging look at two great Jewish philosophers and what their thinking means to our understanding of God, truth, revelation and reason. 6 x 9, 224 pp, HC, 978-1-58023-411-5 **$24.99**

The Death of Death: Resurrection and Immortality in Jewish Thought
By Rabbi Neil Gillman, PhD 6 x 9, 336 pp, Quality PB, 978-1-58023-081-0 **$18.95**

Doing Jewish Theology: God, Torah & Israel in Modern Judaism *By Rabbi Neil Gillman, PhD*
6 x 9, 304 pp, Quality PB, 978-1-58023-439-9 **$18.99**

Hasidic Tales: Annotated & Explained *Translation & Annotation by Rabbi Rami Shapiro*
5½ x 8½, 240 pp, Quality PB, 978-1-893361-86-7 **$16.95***

A Heart of Many Rooms: Celebrating the Many Voices within Judaism
By Dr. David Hartman 6 x 9, 352 pp, Quality PB, 978-1-58023-156-5 **$19.95**

The Hebrew Prophets: Selections Annotated & Explained
Translation & Annotation by Rabbi Rami Shapiro; Foreword by Rabbi Zalman M. Schachter-Shalomi
5½ x 8½, 224 pp, Quality PB, 978-1-59473-037-5 **$16.99***

A Jewish Understanding of the New Testament *By Rabbi Samuel Sandmel; Preface by Rabbi David Sandmel* 5½ x 8½, 368 pp, Quality PB, 978-1-59473-048-1 **$19.99***

Jews and Judaism in the 21st Century: Human Responsibility, the Presence of God and the Future of the Covenant *Edited by Rabbi Edward Feinstein; Foreword by Paula E. Hyman*
6 x 9, 192 pp, Quality PB, 978-1-58023-374-3 **$19.99**

A Living Covenant: The Innovative Spirit in Traditional Judaism
By Dr. David Hartman 6 x 9, 368 pp, Quality PB, 978-1-58023-011-7 **$25.00**

Love and Terror in the God Encounter: The Theological Legacy of Rabbi Joseph B. Soloveitchik *By Dr. David Hartman* 6 x 9, 240 pp, Quality PB, 978-1-58023-176-3 **$19.95**

A Touch of the Sacred: A Theologian's Informal Guide to Jewish Belief
By Dr. Eugene B. Borowitz and Frances W. Schwartz
6 x 9, 256 pp, Quality PB, 978-1-58023-416-0 **$16.99**; HC, 978-1-58023-337-8 **$21.99**

Traces of God: Seeing God in Torah, History and Everyday Life *By Rabbi Neil Gillman, PhD*
6 x 9, 240 pp, Quality PB, 978-1-58023-369-9 **$16.99**

Your Word Is Fire: The Hasidic Masters on Contemplative Prayer
Edited and translated by Rabbi Arthur Green, PhD, and Barry W. Holtz
6 x 9, 160 pp, Quality PB, 978-1-879045-25-5 **$15.95**

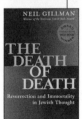

I Am Jewish

Personal Reflections Inspired by the Last Words of Daniel Pearl
Almost 150 Jews—both famous and not—from all walks of life, from all around the world, write about many aspects of their Judaism.
Edited by Judea and Ruth Pearl 6 x 9, 304 pp, Deluxe PB w/ flaps, 978-1-58023-259-3 **$18.99**
Download a free copy of the *I Am Jewish Teacher's Guide* at www.jewishlights.com.

Hannah Senesh: Her Life and Diary, The First Complete Edition
By Hannah Senesh; Foreword by Marge Piercy; Preface by Eitan Senesh; Afterword by Roberta Grossman
6 x 9, 368 pp, b/w photos, Quality PB, 978-1-58023-342-2 **$19.99**

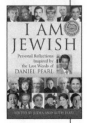

*A book from SkyLight Paths, Jewish Lights' sister imprint

Social Justice

Confronting Scandal
How Jews Can Respond When Jews Do Bad Things
By Dr. Erica Brown

A framework to transform our sense of shame over reports of Jews committing crime into actions that inspire and sustain a moral culture.

6 x 9, 192 pp, HC, 978-1-58023-440-5 **$24.99**

There Shall Be No Needy
Pursuing Social Justice through Jewish Law and Tradition
By Rabbi Jill Jacobs; Foreword by Rabbi Elliot N. Dorff, PhD; Preface by Simon Greer

Confronts the most pressing issues of twenty-first-century America from a deeply Jewish perspective. 6 x 9, 288 pp, Quality PB, 978-1-58023-425-2 **$16.99**

There Shall Be No Needy Teacher's Guide 8½ x 11, 56 pp, PB, 978-1-58023-429-0 **$8.99**

Conscience
The Duty to Obey and the Duty to Disobey
By Rabbi Harold M. Schulweis

Examines the idea of conscience and the role conscience plays in our relationships to government, law, ethics, religion, human nature, God—and to each other.

6 x 9, 160 pp, Quality PB, 978-1-58023-419-1 **$16.99**; HC, 978-1-58023-375-0 **$19.99**

Judaism and Justice
The Jewish Passion to Repair the World
By Rabbi Sidney Schwarz; Foreword by Ruth Messinger

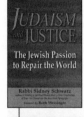

Explores the relationship between Judaism, social justice and the Jewish identity of American Jews. 6 x 9, 352 pp, Quality PB, 978-1-58023-353-8 **$19.99**

Spirituality/Women's Interest

New Jewish Feminism
Probing the Past, Forging the Future
Edited by Rabbi Elyse Goldstein; Foreword by Anita Diamant

Looks at the growth and accomplishments of Jewish feminism and what they mean for Jewish women today and tomorrow.

6 x 9, 480 pp, Quality PB, 978-1-58023-448-1 **$19.99**; HC, 978-1-58023-359-0 **$24.99**

The Divine Feminine in Biblical Wisdom Literature
Selections Annotated & Explained
Translation & Annotation by Rabbi Rami Shapiro
5½ x 8½, 240 pp, Quality PB, 978-1-59473-109-9 **$16.99**
(A book from SkyLight Paths, Jewish Lights' sister imprint)

The Quotable Jewish Woman
Wisdom, Inspiration & Humor from the Mind & Heart
Edited by Elaine Bernstein Partnow
6 x 9, 496 pp, Quality PB, 978-1-58023-236-4 **$19.99**

The Women's Haftarah Commentary
New Insights from Women Rabbis on the 54 Weekly Haftarah Portions, the 5 Megillot & Special Shabbatot
Edited by Rabbi Elyse Goldstein

Illuminates the historical significance of female portrayals in the Haftarah and the Five Megillot. 6 x 9, 560 pp, Quality PB, 978-1-58023-371-2 **$19.99**

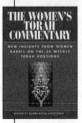

The Women's Torah Commentary
New Insights from Women Rabbis on the 54 Weekly Torah Portions
Edited by Rabbi Elyse Goldstein

Over fifty women rabbis offer inspiring insights on the Torah, in a week-by-week format.

6 x 9, 496 pp, Quality PB, 978-1-58023-370-5 **$19.99**; HC, 978-1-58023-076-6 **$34.95**

See Passover for *The Women's Passover Companion: Women's Reflections on the Festival of Freedom* and *The Women's Seder Sourcebook: Rituals & Readings for Use at the Passover Seder.*

Inspiration

God of Me: Imagining God throughout Your Lifetime
By Rabbi David Lyon Helps you cut through preconceived ideas of God and dogmas that stifle your creativity when thinking about your personal relationship with God. 6 x 9, 176 pp, Quality PB, 978-1-58023-452-8 **$16.99**

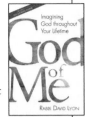

The God Upgrade: Finding Your 21st-Century Spirituality in Judaism's 5,000-Year-Old Tradition *By Rabbi Jamie Korngold; Foreword by Rabbi Harold M. Schulweis* A provocative look at how our changing God concepts have shaped every aspect of Judaism. 6 x 9, 176 pp, Quality PB, 978-1-58023-443-6 **$15.99**

The Seven Questions You're Asked in Heaven: Reviewing and Renewing Your Life on Earth *By Dr. Ron Wolfson* An intriguing and entertaining resource for living a life that matters. 6 x 9, 176 pp, Quality PB, 978-1-58023-407-8 **$16.99**

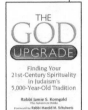

Happiness and the Human Spirit: The Spirituality of Becoming the Best You Can Be *By Rabbi Abraham J. Twerski, MD*
Shows you that true happiness is attainable once you stop looking outside yourself for the source. 6 x 9, 176 pp, Quality PB, 978-1-58023-404-7 **$16.99**; HC, 978-1-58023-343-9 **$19.99**

A Formula for Proper Living: Practical Lessons from Life and Torah
By Rabbi Abraham J. Twerski, MD 6 x 9, 144 pp, HC, 978-1-58023-402-3 **$19.99**

The Bridge to Forgiveness: Stories and Prayers for Finding God and Restoring Wholeness *By Rabbi Karyn D. Kedar* 6 x 9, 176 pp, Quality PB, 978-1-58023-451-1 **$16.99**

The Empty Chair: Finding Hope and Joy—Timeless Wisdom from a Hasidic Master, Rebbe Nachman of Breslov *Adapted by Moshe Mykoff and the Breslov Research Institute*
4 x 6, 128 pp, Deluxe PB w/ flaps, 978-1-879045-67-5 **$9.99**

The Gentle Weapon: Prayers for Everyday and Not-So-Everyday Moments— Timeless Wisdom from the Teachings of the Hasidic Master, Rebbe Nachman of Breslov *Adapted by Moshe Mykoff and S. C. Mizrahi, together with the Breslov Research Institute*
4 x 6, 144 pp, Deluxe PB w/ flaps, 978-1-58023-022-3 **$9.99**

God Whispers: Stories of the Soul, Lessons of the Heart *By Rabbi Karyn D. Kedar*
6 x 9, 176 pp, Quality PB, 978-1-58023-088-9 **$15.95**

God's To-Do List: 103 Ways to Be an Angel and Do God's Work on Earth
By Dr. Ron Wolfson 6 x 9, 144 pp, Quality PB, 978-1-58023-301-9 **$16.99**

Jewish Stories from Heaven and Earth: Inspiring Tales to Nourish the Heart and Soul *Edited by Rabbi Dov Peretz Elkins* 6 x 9, 304 pp, Quality PB, 978-1-58023-363-7 **$16.99**

Life's Daily Blessings: Inspiring Reflections on Gratitude and Joy for Every Day, Based on Jewish Wisdom *By Rabbi Kerry M. Olitzky* 4½ x 6½, 368 pp, Quality PB, 978-1-58023-396-5 **$16.99**

Restful Reflections: Nighttime Inspiration to Calm the Soul, Based on Jewish Wisdom
By Rabbi Kerry M. Olitzky and Rabbi Lori Forman-Jacobi 4½ x 6½, 448 pp, Quality PB, 978-1-58023-091-9 **$15.95**

Sacred Intentions: Morning Inspiration to Strengthen the Spirit, Based on Jewish Wisdom
By Rabbi Kerry M. Olitzky and Rabbi Lori Forman-Jacobi 4½ x 6½, 448 pp, Quality PB, 978-1-58023-061-2 **$16.99**

Kabbalah/Mysticism

Jewish Mysticism and the Spiritual Life: Classical Texts, Contemporary Reflections *Edited by Dr. Lawrence Fine, Dr. Eitan Fishbane and Rabbi Or N. Rose* Inspirational and thought-provoking materials for contemplation, discussion and action. 6 x 9, 256 pp, HC, 978-1-58023-434-4 **$24.99**

Ehyeh: A Kabbalah for Tomorrow
By Rabbi Arthur Green, PhD 6 x 9, 224 pp, Quality PB, 978-1-58023-213-5 **$18.99**

The Gift of Kabbalah: Discovering the Secrets of Heaven, Renewing Your Life on Earth
By Tamar Frankiel, PhD 6 x 9, 256 pp, Quality PB, 978-1-58023-141-1 **$16.95**

Seek My Face: A Jewish Mystical Theology *By Rabbi Arthur Green, PhD*
6 x 9, 304 pp, Quality PB, 978-1-58023-130-5 **$19.95**

Zohar: Annotated & Explained *Translation & Annotation by Dr. Daniel C. Matt; Foreword by Andrew Harvey* 5½ x 8½, 176 pp, Quality PB, 978-1-893361-51-5 **$15.99**
(A book from SkyLight Paths, Jewish Lights' sister imprint)

See also *The Way Into Jewish Mystical Tradition* in The Way Into… Series.

Spirituality

Repentance: The Meaning and Practice of *Teshuvah*
By Dr. Louis E. Newman; Foreword by Rabbi Harold M. Schulweis; Preface by Rabbi Karyn D. Kedar
Examines both the practical and philosophical dimensions of *teshuvah*, Judaism's core religious-moral teaching on repentance, and its value for us—Jews and non-Jews alike—today. 6 x 9, 256 pp, HC, 978-1-58023-426-9 **$24.99**

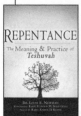

Tanya, the Masterpiece of Hasidic Wisdom
Selections Annotated & Explained
Translation & Annotation by Rabbi Rami Shapiro; Foreword by Rabbi Zalman M. Schachter-Shalomi
Brings the genius of *Tanya*, one of the most powerful books of Jewish wisdom, to anyone seeking to deepen their understanding of the soul.
5½ x 8½, 240 pp, Quality PB, 978-1-59473-275-1 **$16.99**
(A book from SkyLight Paths, Jewish Lights' sister imprint)

Aleph-Bet Yoga: Embodying the Hebrew Letters for Physical and Spiritual Well-Being
By Steven A. Rapp; Foreword by Tamar Frankiel, PhD, and Judy Greenfeld; Preface by Hart Lazer
7 x 10, 128 pp, b/w photos, Quality PB, Lay-flat binding, 978-1-58023-162-6 **$16.95**

A Book of Life: Embracing Judaism as a Spiritual Practice
By Rabbi Michael Strassfeld 6 x 9, 544 pp, Quality PB, 978-1-58023-247-0 **$19.99**

Bringing the Psalms to Life: How to Understand and Use the Book of Psalms
By Rabbi Daniel F. Polish, PhD 6 x 9, 208 pp, Quality PB, 978-1-58023-157-2 **$16.95**

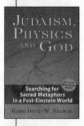

Does the Soul Survive? A Jewish Journey to Belief in Afterlife, Past Lives & Living with Purpose *By Rabbi Elie Kaplan Spitz; Foreword by Brian L. Weiss, MD*
6 x 9, 288 pp, Quality PB, 978-1-58023-165-7 **$16.99**

First Steps to a New Jewish Spirit: Reb Zalman's Guide to Recapturing the Intimacy & Ecstasy in Your Relationship with God *By Rabbi Zalman M. Schachter-Shalomi with Donald Gropman* 6 x 9, 144 pp, Quality PB, 978-1-58023-182-4 **$16.95**

Foundations of Sephardic Spirituality: The Inner Life of Jews of the Ottoman Empire
By Rabbi Marc D. Angel, PhD 6 x 9, 224 pp, Quality PB, 978-1-58023-341-5 **$18.99**

God & the Big Bang: Discovering Harmony between Science & Spirituality
By Dr. Daniel C. Matt 6 x 9, 216 pp, Quality PB, 978-1-879045-89-7 **$16.99**

God in Our Relationships: Spirituality between People from the Teachings of Martin Buber *By Rabbi Dennis S. Ross* 5½ x 8½, 160 pp, Quality PB, 978-1-58023-147-3 **$16.95**

The Jewish Lights Spirituality Handbook: A Guide to Understanding, Exploring & Living a Spiritual Life *Edited by Stuart M. Matlins*
What exactly is "Jewish" about spirituality? How do I make it a part of my life? Fifty of today's foremost spiritual leaders share their ideas and experience with us.
6 x 9, 456 pp, Quality PB, 978-1-58023-093-3 **$19.99**

Judaism, Physics and God: Searching for Sacred Metaphors in a Post-Einstein World
By Rabbi David W. Nelson 6 x 9, 352 pp, Quality PB, inc. reader's discussion guide, 978-1-58023-306-4 **$18.99**; HC, 352 pp, 978-1-58023-252-4 **$24.99**

Meaning & Mitzvah: Daily Practices for Reclaiming Judaism through Prayer, God, Torah, Hebrew, Mitzvot and Peoplehood *By Rabbi Goldie Milgram*
7 x 9, 336 pp, Quality PB, 978-1-58023-256-2 **$19.99**

Minding the Temple of the Soul: Balancing Body, Mind, and Spirit through Traditional Jewish Prayer, Movement, and Meditation *By Tamar Frankiel, PhD, and Judy Greenfeld*
7 x 10, 184 pp, Illus., Quality PB, 978-1-879045-64-4 **$18.99**

One God Clapping: The Spiritual Path of a Zen Rabbi *By Rabbi Alan Lew with Sherril Jaffe*
5½ x 8½, 336 pp, Quality PB, 978-1-58023-115-2 **$16.95**

The Soul of the Story: Meetings with Remarkable People
By Rabbi David Zeller 6 x 9, 288 pp, HC, 978-1-58023-272-2 **$21.99**

There Is No Messiah ... and You're It: The Stunning Transformation of Judaism's Most Provocative Idea *By Rabbi Robert N. Levine, DD*
6 x 9, 192 pp, Quality PB, 978-1-58023-255-5 **$16.99**

These Are the Words: A Vocabulary of Jewish Spiritual Life
By Rabbi Arthur Green, PhD 6 x 9, 304 pp, Quality PB, 978-1-58023-107-7 **$18.95**

Spirituality/Prayer

Making Prayer Real: Leading Jewish Spiritual Voices on Why Prayer Is Difficult and What to Do about It *By Rabbi Mike Comins*
A new and different response to the challenges of Jewish prayer, with "best prayer practices" from Jewish spiritual leaders of all denominations.
6 x 9, 320 pp, Quality PB, 978-1-58023-417-7 **$18.99**

Witnesses to the One: The Spiritual History of the *Sh'ma*
By Rabbi Joseph B. Meszler; Foreword by Rabbi Elyse Goldstein
6 x 9, 176 pp, Quality PB, 978-1-58023-400-9 **$16.99**; HC, 978-1-58023-309-5 **$19.99**

My People's Prayer Book Series: Traditional Prayers, Modern Commentaries *Edited by Rabbi Lawrence A. Hoffman, PhD*
Provides diverse and exciting commentary to the traditional liturgy. Will help you find new wisdom in Jewish prayer, and bring liturgy into your life. Each book includes Hebrew text, modern translations and commentaries from all perspectives of the Jewish world.

Vol. 1—The *Sh'ma* and Its Blessings
   7 x 10, 168 pp, HC, 978-1-879045-79-8 **$29.99**
Vol. 2—The *Amidah* 7 x 10, 240 pp, HC, 978-1-879045-80-4 **$24.95**
Vol. 3—*P'sukei D'zimrah* (Morning Psalms)
   7 x 10, 240 pp, HC, 978-1-879045-81-1 **$29.99**
Vol. 4—*Seder K'riat Hatorah* (The Torah Service)
   7 x 10, 264 pp, HC, 978-1-879045-82-8 **$29.99**
Vol. 5—*Birkhot Hashachar* (Morning Blessings)
   7 x 10, 240 pp, HC, 978-1-879045-83-5 **$24.95**
Vol. 6—*Tachanun* and Concluding Prayers
   7 x 10, 240 pp, HC, 978-1-879045-84-2 **$24.95**
Vol. 7—Shabbat at Home 7 x 10, 240 pp, HC, 978-1-879045-85-9 **$24.95**
Vol. 8—*Kabbalat Shabbat* (Welcoming Shabbat in the Synagogue)
   7 x 10, 240 pp, HC, 978-1-58023-121-3 **$24.99**
Vol. 9—Welcoming the Night: *Minchah* and *Ma'ariv* (Afternoon and
   Evening Prayer) 7 x 10, 272 pp, HC, 978-1-58023-262-3 **$24.99**
Vol. 10—Shabbat Morning: *Shacharit* and *Musaf* (Morning and
   Additional Services) 7 x 10, 240 pp, HC, 978-1-58023-240-1 **$29.99**

Spirituality/Lawrence Kushner

I'm God; You're Not: Observations on Organized Religion & Other Disguises of the Ego
6 x 9, 256 pp, HC, 978-1-58023-441-2 **$21.99**

The Book of Letters: A Mystical Hebrew Alphabet
Popular HC Edition, 6 x 9, 80 pp, 2-color text, 978-1-879045-00-2 **$24.95**
Collector's Limited Edition, 9 x 12, 80 pp, gold-foil-embossed pages, w/ limited-edition silkscreened print, 978-1-879045-04-0 **$349.00**

The Book of Miracles: A Young Person's Guide to Jewish Spiritual Awareness
6 x 9, 96 pp, 2-color illus., HC, 978-1-879045-78-1 **$16.95** *For ages 9–13*

The Book of Words: Talking Spiritual Life, Living Spiritual Talk
6 x 9, 160 pp, Quality PB, 978-1-58023-020-9 **$18.99**

Eyes Remade for Wonder: A Lawrence Kushner Reader *Introduction by Thomas Moore*
6 x 9, 240 pp, Quality PB, 978-1-58023-042-1 **$18.95**

God Was in This Place & I, i Did Not Know: Finding Self, Spirituality and Ultimate Meaning 6 x 9, 192 pp, Quality PB, 978-1-879045-33-0 **$16.95**

Honey from the Rock: An Introduction to Jewish Mysticism
6 x 9, 176 pp, Quality PB, 978-1-58023-073-5 **$16.95**

Invisible Lines of Connection: Sacred Stories of the Ordinary
5½ x 8½, 160 pp, Quality PB, 978-1-879045-98-9 **$15.95**

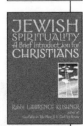

Jewish Spirituality: A Brief Introduction for Christians
5½ x 8½, 112 pp, Quality PB, 978-1-58023-150-3 **$12.95**

The River of Light: Jewish Mystical Awareness
6 x 9, 192 pp, Quality PB, 978-1-58023-096-4 **$16.95**

The Way Into Jewish Mystical Tradition
6 x 9, 224 pp, Quality PB, 978-1-58023-200-5 **$18.99**; HC, 978-1-58023-029-2 **$21.95**

About Jewish Lights

People of all faiths and backgrounds yearn for books that attract, engage, educate, and spiritually inspire.

Our principal goal is to stimulate thought and help all people learn about who the Jewish People are, where they come from, and what the future can be made to hold. While people of our diverse Jewish heritage are the primary audience, our books speak to people in the Christian world as well and will broaden their understanding of Judaism and the roots of their own faith.

We bring to you authors who are at the forefront of spiritual thought and experience. While each has something different to say, they all say it in a voice that you can hear.

Our books are designed to welcome you and then to engage, stimulate, and inspire. We judge our success not only by whether or not our books are beautiful and commercially successful, but by whether or not they make a difference in your life.

For your information and convenience, at the back of this book we have provided a list of other Jewish Lights books you might find interesting and useful. They cover all the categories of your life:

Bar/Bat Mitzvah
Bible Study / Midrash
Children's Books
Congregation Resources
Current Events / History
Ecology / Environment
Fiction: Mystery, Science Fiction
Grief / Healing
Holidays / Holy Days
Inspiration
Kabbalah / Mysticism / Enneagram

Life Cycle
Meditation
Men's Interest
Parenting
Prayer / Ritual / Sacred Practice
Social Justice
Spirituality
Theology / Philosophy
Travel
Twelve Steps
Women's Interest

Stuart M. Matlins

Stuart M. Matlins, Publisher

Or phone, fax, mail or e-mail to: **JEWISH LIGHTS Publishing**
Sunset Farm Offices, Route 4 • P.O. Box 237 • Woodstock, Vermont 05091
Tel: (802) 457-4000 • Fax: (802) 457-4004 • www.jewishlights.com
Credit card orders: (800) 962-4544 (8:30AM–5:30PM ET Monday–Friday)
Generous discounts on quantity orders. SATISFACTION GUARANTEED. Prices subject to change.

For more information about each book, visit our website at www.jewishlights.com